CHANNEL ISLAND MONSTERS

ERREN MICHAELS

ILLUSTRATED BY AMELIA WILDE

The
History
Press

For my Dad

First published 2023

The History Press
97 St George's Place, Cheltenham,
Gloucestershire, GL50 3QB
www.thehistorypress.co.uk

British Library Cataloguing in Publication Data.
A catalogue record for this book is available from the British Library.

ISBN 978 1 80399 472 7

Typesetting and origination by The History Press
Printed and bound in Great Britain by TJ Books Limited, Padstow, Cornwall.

Trees for LYfe

INTRODUCTION

The monsters in this book sharpened their claws and scared children long before literacy was commonplace, or books were available. The mythology of the Channel Islands originates in spoken storytelling. If there was an original child who ran crying from their room to tell their parents that they had just seen *Lé Croque-Mitaine's* long claws curl over their windowsill, it was not written down anywhere. There must have been one parent, before any other, who earnestly warned of *La Cocangne* whispering down the well, to make their child stay away from the edge. The parent has been forgotten, but the monster survived through history because other parents told their children, who who repeated it to their own children, on and on across the centuries. Perhaps there was a single smuggler who had the idea to run into a crowded inn one night and shout that he had just encountered a giant black dog, a mighty beast with hellfire eyes stalking the night. The black dogs remain. The smuggler is forgotten, even if his trick to move illicit cargo ashore became common practice.

Some monsters stayed well-known. Their tales were re-spun by naturally gifted tellers of bedtime stories, or in drunk and earnest groups in smoky taverns, over and over. Sometimes stories would have been told seriously as warnings. Sometimes to entertain by candlelight on long winter evenings. Whether or not people believed the legends, the monsters of the islands thrived within them for generations.

Stories, like the magical creatures who inhabit them, can be immortal. They have a life and a will of their own. They slip through centuries, forever young, changing with the teller and adapting to their audiences. In these islands sirens sang and storm witches roared, and ships were smashed into hidden rocks by seething tides as treacherous as any in the world. Monsters underwent metamorphosis in the retelling, growing stronger. In a culture of storytelling, visiting sailors shared their own tales. The sailors may have left, but their stories stayed, and so did their monsters.

The story heritage of the Channel Islands was once rich and colourful. It was woven for so long by its people, by their character and history and humour, into a web of legends stretching over the beautiful and dangerous geography of the islands.

Then it began to die.

The old stories had been retold in the native island languages, Jèrriais and Guernésiais, which are now spoken by only a few hundred people. As the languages of the island were forgotten, so was the mythology carried within it. There were many long years during which even mentioning magic or monsters could lead to accusations of witchcraft, so repeating legends became dangerous. Literacy and the rise of the novel brought new stories, and an easier way to enjoy them. Roads were cut through lonely places and there were lanterns to light the darkness. While no islander in their right mind would walk the Forest Road at night, or scramble up Crack-Ankle Lane after sunset, there was suddenly less interest in myths and legends.

As their stories were no longer told, the monsters of the Channel Islands lived on only in fading recollections. They lingered sadly in the places named for them. They slinked back to what was left of the dark woods and were mostly forgotten. Sometimes monsters were confined, all stripped of detail, into the texts of old guidebooks which described them as 'folklore' or 'superstitions'. They were dismissed as old wives' tales or fairy stories, suitable only for little children. They became the quaint curiosities of a dying culture. Electric lights blazed and monsters receded into the shadows. Some were lost forever. They dissipated in the last moment that their story was remembered and were silently devoured by time.

Some waited quietly. They had dug their claws into those places named after them, and into the academic work of those few wise people who realised that the history of a place and its people lives as much in the ephemera of its stories, folklore and traditions as it does in its ancient standing stones and castles.

It is possible that some Channel Island legends have existed for longer than anything that is solid and tangible, or built from stone, other than the dolmens. The mystery of why there are so many 'Fairy-Stone' dolmens in the islands is as unlikely to be solved as the question: why *do* such little islands have such a vast trove of stories about fairies and monsters? The mythology of the landscape is almost ludicrously crowded with fantastic creatures. Any poor, superstitious fisherman of the last few centuries must have feared that he would struggle to avoid the wrath of storm witches, sirens and sea monsters. Even if he made it back to land, past the kelpies and selkies near the shore, he was unlikely to get far on the path home without being eaten by a variety of mythical creatures, or struck dead by the glance of one of the giant black dogs that people kept mentioning in the taverns. He may have considered it quite fortunate that so much cheap alcohol was mysteriously available on the island, because at least he could afford to drink his fears away.

Every creature in this book has been part of the fabric of folklore within the islands for a very long time. Some are unique to a specific island. Some of them inhabit more than one island. Others prefer the water in between. Some monsters only survived in scraps of information or in contradictory accounts. The monsters in this book may very well wake up in these stories, shake the dust off their claws, and discover that their tale is different to how they remember it. That it's being told in a different language, and they don't like how they look in their picture, or how their name is pronounced, or why everyone makes such a fuss now when somebody gets eaten.

Far too much detail has been lost to know how these tales may have been told in centuries past. Changes, sometimes quite dramatic ones, have always been the nature of folklore and fairytales. They are a living litany of bald-faced lies and outlandish claims just as much as they are careful constructions or recounting of memories. It is pointless to try and pull threads from the weave to see what might be considered 'real'. Many versions exist. Many versions have been lost. This book is just one adaptation of these tales.

Evolution is always better than the alternative. Stories left untold are stories that die, and when folklore is lost, a thread winding back through generations of storytellers snaps forever.

A valuable heritage hides in stories of myths and magic. There are shades of all the people who passed stories onto others. There are echoes of the recitals of thousands of voices and their thoughtful alterations made in telling and retelling. From the changes made by booming oral storytellers seeking ringing rhythms to enchant crowds, to the careful omissions made by parents for the ears of their children. There are even shadows of truths stuttered out by men or women scared witless by the things they saw, or thought they saw, in dark and lonely places.

The mythology of the islands is a gift passed down to everyone. It grows stronger in being shared. It is an inheritance that links each listener, each reader, back to those who came before. Surely that is proof, if anything can be, that there is a little bit of magic in the world.

LA COCANGNE

Aqueous nymphs, or nixes, yclept Grindylow and Jenny Greenteeth,
lurked at the bottom of pits, and with their long sinewy arms
dragged in and drowned children venturing too near.

John Higson

Cassie sat against the wall of the little cave and drew her knees up. She hugged them to her chest with a sigh and rested her head on them, looking out into the daylight from the shadows.

It was quiet here in the well-cave, since most of the water drawing happened early in the morning, and she could watch all the people of the castle walk by, since it was located on the main path that ran from the top to the bottom of the vast stone fortress.

It was an odd place for a well, she thought. So high above the ground. This level of the castle was already higher than the rooftops of the fancy town houses where Cassie wished that she and her family lived. Or at least, she *had* wished that, until she had seen the fletcher's boy Flynn. After that, she had decided she didn't mind so much living in a castle, far away from the shops where they sold pretty dresses and sweets and ribbons.

While Cassie enjoyed the sheltered privacy of the cave, she did not much like the well itself. She had leaned over the edge once, when they had first arrived. The gaping darkness had pulled at her, making her feel like she might fall.

'That's just your instincts telling you to keep back,' her father had said, when she told him of the horrible feeling, 'That's to keep you safe, my dear.'

He had rubbed his ink-stained fingers thoughtfully and then smiled. 'I should get back to work. Wait! Pass me that green pigment, but don't get it on your dress for goodness' sake.'

So immersed was Cassie in her thoughts of Flynn, that it was a while before she realised that the soft echoes of the well had taken on a sing-song quality, and that the voice on the edge of her hearing was coming from inside, not outside, the cave.

She sat up stiff and put her hands to the cold stone floor.

'Wishes, riches, power of witches; faery magic, goblin gold, secrets, beauty, joy untold…'

'Hello?' Cassie said.

The voice was strange and distracted, like an old woman who had wondered from her room and forgotten what she was saying.

'La Cocangne in the well. Granting a wish, casting a spell.'

Cassie tilted her head towards the voice as it continued.

'The price of a coin, the touch of hand, for all the magic in this land…'

She scrambled to her knees and crept closer.

'A chance that's granted to a few – reach out your hand, it shall be you.'

'Hello?' Cassie called again.

'Hello, hello, no one we know, no men with buckets who come and go, their days all orders, chores and habit, they don't deserve a wish or magic…'

'Are you *in the well?*' Cassie asked. 'Did you fall in? Do you need help down there?'

She shuffled almost to the edge of the well, but was too nervous to peer in. 'Do you always speak in poetry?'

'Questions, questions, cheeky whelp! The well's my home, I don't need help. And yes, I weave words all the time, the magic lives within the rhyme. Come closer, let me see your face… a pretty thing within this place. A coin, or kiss, shall grant your wish. Speak clear and loud and clasp my hand, the most powerful magic in all–'

'I need a coin!' Cassie jumped to her feet and raced away.

She didn't have a coin. Why would she? And her father had certainly raised her better than to kiss strange faeries, which had seemed to be the other choice. Besides, girls in true love never kissed anybody *except* their true love, and she was quite certain that her true love was Flynn the fletcher's boy.

Grabbing the hem of her dress, she raced up the long flight of stone stairs at a swift, high-kneed trot that made her pigtails bounce and lash around her face. She was out of breath by the time she reached the residential area of the castle, where her steps became noisier on wooden floorboards.

She darted through rooms that had seemed a maze when she had first arrived there. Along passages switching back and forth against the rock, upstairs, downstairs, until she came to the little room she shared with her sister, and out of breath shouted, 'Isobel! Give me a coin!'

Several minutes later, and no closer to getting a coin, Cassie had stamped her foot twice and was shouting again. Isobel, ever the picture of ladylike calm, was still leaning back against her pillows with her book resting against her raised knees.

'Cassie, really. Somebody is making fun of you. Waiting to laugh at you throwing your father's money down a damp hole for a wish that won't come true. Faeries and wishing wells indeed! Whoever heard of such a thing?'

'*Everybody*, Isobel.' Cassie stamped her foot again enjoying the loud bang. 'Everybody has heard of faeries and wishing wells and magic. Especially in these islands. The soldiers all say that the Channel Islands are very magical, and that there are doors to another land and – do not snort at me Isobel! I've heard them say so! Real, grown-up men!'

'I did not snort,' Isobel exclaimed, losing her calm for the first time. 'I merely sighed with vigour. I am a young lady and I have never snorted in my life.'

'You did snort. You snorted like a pig! Now give me a coin, you self-ish witch. I want to make myself a wish. There, now I'm rhyming too.'

'You can't make a wish,' said Isobel slamming her book shut, 'because it's dinnertime.'

Cassie realised the logic of this statement at the precise moment that she realised she was hungry, and suffered herself to be tidied by her older sister and then led to the dining hall.

She had not forgotten the faery, and sweetly asked her father for a coin.

When he asked her, bemused, what she needed money for, she decided honesty was the best policy and told him that she wanted to make a wish in the well. Satisfied with this explanation he counted out two little copper coins and pushed them along the table.

'There's one for you too, Isobel,' their father said with a smile. 'Wish for something nice.'

'Look, Cassie,' Isobel whispered, as she passed the money to her sister. 'Even his coins have map ink on them. We'll go down tomorrow.'

As the midnight bell struck Cassie slipped out from under her covers and, as quietly as she could, put her dress back on over her shift. She groped blindly in the dark for her shoes, and carried them with her, wincing when she banged them against the door as she turned the handle and crept out.

She moved away from her room before putting her shoes on. She had carefully left the coin in her right shoe so that she didn't have to search for it in the dark. She began walking as though she had every right to be up and about at this time, with her head high and a prim expression on her face.

She slipped out of the large, iron-bound door of the keep, and the soldiers stationed on either side looked at her curiously. She recognised the one with freckles – his name was Bry. Neither he nor the older man questioned her, so she scampered swiftly down the stone stairs, the cool night air feeling chill against her flushed cheeks. The coin dug into her palm as she clutched it tight, terrified that she might drop it and hear it ping away into the shadows. She skipped down the last of the steps and hesitated before the mouth of the cave. The flaming torch at the entrance cast light which did not reach as far back as the well. Cassie stepped blinking into the blackness and peered towards where she knew the mouth of the well waited in the dark.

'Hello?' she whispered. 'Are you still there, faery person? I have a coin now.'

For a moment there was nothing, then she heard something far and deep. Echoes of whispers. Muttered words blending and merging, slowly getting louder.

Cassie felt suddenly disorientated in the darkness and she moved sideways until her hand touched the wall. She did not move closer to the well.

'She comes in darkness, comes at night, she stays in shadows out of sight, without a fire without a light, she needs a wish to make things right.'

'Yes please,' said Cassie as the voice echoed closer. 'My father gave me a coin to make a wish.' She swallowed her fear and added, 'It's only a copper coin. I hope that is enough. Do I throw it in? Is it like a wishing well?'

There was the soft pattering of water dripping onto the floor as the whispering voice filled the room, and Cassie shivered to think of the faery living so deep and dark in the water of the well.

'Take a step, and do not pause, take my hand… your wish is yours!'

Cassie thought of how cold and wet that hand must be. She wondered what manner of faery would live at the bottom of a well.

'And I can wish for *anything* at all?' she asked.

'It's all your choice, just use your voice, speak your desire… you think me a liar?'

'Oh no! Of course not,' Cassie took a slow step forward, eyes straining to see a shape in the black. She thought perhaps she could make out the line of a hairless head, a figure even smaller than she was. Outside, the torchlight flickered in the breeze and its eyes shone. They were pale and luminous and, as she hesitated, they narrowed. Somewhere on the night breeze, Cassie heard voices.

'My patience wanes. My magic drains. I made my climb. Don't waste my time.'

'No! No, I'm sorry. I wish… I wish that the fletcher's boy… No. Wait. I wish that everybody I love stayed safe and happy until they grow old and die. Is that… Is that something you can grant?'

'Pay your sum… and the deal is done.'

Cassie stepped forward, her coin held out between her finger and thumb, to where the gleam of light had caught the faery's eyes. She dreaded the feeling of its cold skin brushing against her when it took the coin.

The contact, when it came, was upon her wrist. Cold, hard fingers closed around her like a shackle and long claws scratched her skin. She cried out as the faery tugged her towards the well. She almost lost her footing as she was pulled against the low edge. Her free hand grabbed at the rough stone in the pitch black. She heard the coin ring against the walls of the well as it bounced down and down, so deep that she didn't even hear it hit the water.

'What are you doing?' she gasped. It was a few moments more until she realised, struggling against the strength of the thing, exactly what it meant to do. She screamed then. A sharp single explosion of panic that rang incredibly loud in the confined space. The faery was pulling her into the well and the endless cold, dark drop. Panic fuelled Cassie's struggles as she tried to shake loose her hand. The monster's thin wet arm looped around her neck. It was horribly strong.

'A long way down… until you drown.'

The thing laughed, a horrible raw, wet sound. She could feel herself teetering, her weight starting to shift, pulled forward against her will. She screamed again, a long hopeless wail. Then there were narrow arms around her waist, dragging her back. They pulled with greater strength, and another voice was screaming along with hers, a voice she knew so well that tears burst from her eyes to hear her sister take a breath near her ear and then screech, 'Somebody help us!'

They struggled, monster and sister, Cassie pulled between them like a prize.

The faery pulled at her arms, clawing her skin, and Cassie thought that surely she and Isobel would lose. Her body was pulled out over the well. She felt more than saw the dark depths yawning beneath her.

Then there was merciful light, and the sound of men shouting. She saw the faery lit by the lantern they carried. Its monstrous face was filled with teeth, its narrowed eyes reflecting light. Its skin was green as pondweed and there was fury in its face as it hissed and dived away.

Arms larger and stronger than her sister's lifted Cassie and carried her outside. She heard the swearing of the guards. Cassie sobbed hysterical laughter to hear Isobel exclaim, in her ladylike fashion, 'If you please, sir, I do not wish to be manhandled!'

The next day they sat in the sun, a stone's throw from the well cave. In the shadows of the cave, two men had been lowered on ropes to find the thing that had attacked the mapmaker's daughters.

'I knew you'd snuck out. You made more noise than a blind cow,' Isobel told her.

'Then what took you so long?' Cassie snapped.

Isobel tidied her skirts in deliberate affectation. 'Unlike you I wasn't prepared to run around the castle half-dressed, like a hoyden, in the dead of night. I don't know what those guards must have thought of you.'

'Don't be a such a prig, Isobel,' Cassie frowned at the cave. 'I don't know how anybody could stand to go down there. In that darkness, with the sides closing in around you and the little circle of light at the top getting smaller and smaller. Knowing that thing is down there. The thought makes me sick.'

'They have to find it, don't they? We can't very well have a monster running around the place. Not to mention, everybody drinks that water. Now *that* makes me feel sick. Months we've been drinking out of that well. Bathing in it. Washing our faces in it. Revolting.'

A figure emerged from the cave and strode towards them. Flynn the fletcher's boy, Cassie realised, and felt her cheeks flame.

'They're bringing the men up now,' he said, crouching down in front of them and smiling. 'No sign of anything down there.'

'Did they check under the water?' Cassie demanded.

'Under the water? Well, no. How could they?'

Isobel sighed and smoothed her skirts again. 'I shall just have to drink wine,' she said.

One of the guards from the night before came to stand with them, and Cassie could see her own worry etched on his face. He knelt and took her hand, turning it so that he could better see the scratches on her arm. His own hand had a bandage where he had been bitten.

'It's still down there, hiding under the water,' Cassie said to him firmly. 'Waiting. Waiting for somebody to lean over and hear it whispering and rhyming, so it can pull them in. It said it could grant wishes…'

'Wishes?' The guard shook his head. 'Unless you wished to be dragged down a well and eaten, I'm pretty sure that thing wasn't granting any wishes.'

'You said it was small, Bry? And green?' Flynn pursed his lips. 'It was probably a Cocangne, then. Mum used to warn us when we were children. Don't lean over the well or the Cocangne will get you,' he wiggled his fingers. 'Scary monster. That sort of thing.'

'It *was* a scary monster,' Isobel said. 'I never heard of such a horrid thing. Pulling people down wells, if you please. How rude.'

'Cocangnes,' Bry narrowed his eyes. 'Isn't there a really big one in Guernsey that lives in a pond out East? I think it has a road named after it. You must have heard that story, Flynn! It eats cats and seagulls when it can't get children, but it definitely prefers children.'

'I don't know anything about Guernsey,' Flynn shook his head, then stood and stretched. 'I tell you what, though – it wouldn't hurt to throw a few sharp rocks down that well from time to time. Keep that nasty little monster on its toes. Maybe we could do that tomorrow?'

'Oh yes!' said Cassie.

'Certainly not,' said Isobel. 'I would not sink to such vulgarity. I believe I shall ask that they put a lid on that well. A lady can't be expected to sleep in a castle where there are monsters roaming about the place trying to eat one's sister. Come along Cassie. I do believe it's time we had some breakfast.'

Smiling at Flynn, Cassie let her sister take her hand and lead her away.

THE MERMAID

I have seen them riding seaward on the waves
Combing the white hair of the waves blown back
When the wind blows the water white and black.

T. S. Eliot

Those wishing to hear of giant squid or leviathan in the incalculable depths of a cold black ocean should look elsewhere than the Channel Islands. Their seas are shallow and swift, like a silken sheet pulled across a bed of nails. The tides advance and retreat faster and wilder than river rapids, and the sea level rises and falls more dramatically than anywhere else on earth.

Before the famous lighthouse was built in Jersey, the area of lethal rocks known as Corbiere was a site of frequent shipwrecks. After storms, when news of a shipwreck reached them, people would gather on the beach. Some would search for survivors, but most would look for any valuables that might have washed ashore.

One such morning, as the sea receded, it left in its wake the shattered hull of a merchant ship, torn sails still whipping from its broken mast. The sands of the bay had been scoured by earlier arrivals, so Sylvain left the beach in the hope of finding something in the rock pools around Corbiere. He hopped from one low rock to another, his arms out for balance, wavering like an uncertain bird on the wind, trying not to slip on the dark, uneven stone.

Sylvain's lips were grim. He did not like searching the flotsam of a shipwreck, but could not afford the luxury of overlooking some small item that might be sold or exchanged for food. He had sole care of his mother, and her health had been poor for some time.

The wind, the last tatters of the storm, blew his sun-bleached hair into his eyes and battered his worn shirt against his narrow torso.

A bruised apple, bobbing in a rock pool, was his first find. It was last year's harvest, the skin wrinkled, and salt water mixed with the sweet crunch. Perhaps it was from a spilled cargo of apples and cider then. Probably a boat heading away from the islands. Sylvain closed his eyes, savouring the taste as the wind whipped his hair around his ears. He ate the whole thing, core included, and licked the last of the juice and salt from his fingertips.

He continued scrambling over the rocks, using his hands where necessary to keep him upright. The barnacles were rough as broken glass on the palms of his hands. He spotted another apple, scratched but whole, and jammed it in his pocket for his mother.

His search led him further from the shore. Even now, with the tide at its lowest, a lifetime of warnings kept him glancing at the sea. He slipped on the smooth slope of a rock and shouted in annoyance as he slid into a pool, feet first and ankle deep. The water soaked through the holes of his worn-out boots. He sloshed out, sighed, and realised that he may as well continue to wade through the shallow pools now that his feet were wet. He was still cautious in case he lost his footing on the slick green seaweed and drench the rest of himself.

He eyed the sea once more. It was easy to lose track of time. Once the tide turned, it would reach glittering fingers of water through the maze of rocks, pouring into shallow pools, filling them and overflowing faster than a man could scramble.

Sylvain reassured himself that the line of blue water had not advanced. Then he squinted as something glittered. He shaded his eyes and headed towards it through a wide, shallow pool. He found the remains of a smashed apple, held together by its browned skin. Three more were battered but edible. Sylvain was momentarily baffled by how he could carry the apples and still use his hands to scramble over the rocks. Then he smiled, pulled his shirt off over his head and used it to tie a makeshift bag for his meagre haul.

Another sparkle, and now a movement, drew Sylvain's gaze to the same place as before. He knew he should leave. Scrambling towards the sea, seeking unknown treasure, would be foolish. Yet now that he knew exactly where to look, he could see a curve of something orange in the centre of a pool. Perhaps it was a bolt of fabric, or sunlight gleaming on a brown glass bottle.

'I'm probably climbing towards the sea for a broken bottle and some pretty seaweed,' Sylvain muttered to himself as he began to make his slow, careful way closer. 'Stupid. Even if there's a bottle of cider, I'll probably fall over and smash it…'

He stopped as the glittering thing moved. Then there was the unmistakably human gesture of an elegant hand lifted, weakly grasping at a rock before falling away.

Suddenly Sylvain was running, scrambling, his shirt and apples dropped and forgotten, calling out, 'I'm here! I'm coming! *N'inquietez pas, Mademoiselle! Je vais vous aider!*'

How many people had the boat been carrying? He had no idea what language they might speak, but here must be one of its passengers who had survived. A woman in beautiful orange and red skirts. She did not answer him and turned away in an undulating curve as though afraid.

'You do not need to be scared, Miss. I won't hurt you!' He was close enough now that he barely had to raise his voice. 'Do you speak English? I will help you, wherever you are from.'

Sylvain slipped and stumbled to the edge of the pool and dropped to his knees in astonishment. He had been raised by the sea. He had heard the ancient legends of a mermaid caught in fishing nets, and the sailors who had spent too long arguing whether she should be killed or sold, giving her time to cut her way free and dive back to freedom.

The woman here was not what he had imagined, nor what had been described to him in stories. Human skin shimmered down into delicate scales. Mackerel stripes on her arms and flanks, carnelian and coral scales the colour of a winter sunset. What he had mistaken for the skirts of a dress was the swirling membrane of a great tail.

They stared at each other, and there was terror in her limpid eyes, which were as turquoise as a sunlit sea. Gills flared at her neck, but she breathed too, her lips parted in fear.

Ropes of pearls wound around her wrists. A gold comb pinned one side of her copper-coloured hair. The glitter of her jewellery was nothing compared to the living gleam of her tail as it flexed and curled in the shallow pool. Grazes had torn her skin and scales, and one of her high cheekbones was swelling with a purple bruise. The force of the storm had caught more than human victims it seemed. She must have been thrown against the rocks and stranded, helpless, by a receding tide.

She was a living fortune, a beautiful monster, and a woman in need of help.

'Can you understand me?' Sylvain asked quietly.

For a moment she just looked at him, then gave a slow nod.

'Good. That's good.' Sylvain bit his lip then asked, 'You're hurt?'

Another slow, considered nod, a slight narrowing of the eyes.

'Do you need help?'

He thought about the sea rising, rushing into this churning jagged bed of stone knives and how she would be dragged across the rocks. The water too shallow to swim, too powerful for her to cling safely in one place.

'You do need help,' he said more decisively, and leaned forward.

She flinched and swallowed, eyes glancing to his legs, but then nodded.

'My name is Sylvain,' he said. 'Can you… *do* you speak? May I know your name?'

She spoke, and the sound was like wind over the ocean.

'Is that…?' he laughed. 'Was that your *name?*'

She gave a nod and the suggestion of a smile, with pearly white teeth and sharp little fangs.

'I'll call you Neela. I think that's as close as I'll get,' he said.

'Call me as you wish, Sylvain.'

In her voice, his name sounded like a wave whispering onto shore, or a breeze against his neck.

'You said that you would help me,' she unfurled her tail. 'Will you still help me now?'

'Of course,' he said without hesitation.

'I need to get back to the sea,' she said.

'I'll have to carry you then,' Sylvain could feel himself beginning to blush as he moved forward. They were both tense as he slid his arms beneath her. She put her arm around him, and it was cool against his sun-warmed back. He realised how easily she could sink her sharp fangs into his throat. Instead, she held onto him as he lifted her carefully. She was heavy and real. The scent of seawater in her hair.

They made slow progress at first, over uneven rocks and little pools. She was wide-eyed and nervous in his arms. Staring at him with fascination. Sylvain realised how unnerving it must be for a creature of the sea to be held in the air.

'I'm not going to drop you,' Sylvain said as he carried her over a stretch of dry, flat stone. He slipped a little, almost at the same moment he said it, and Neela gripped him so tightly her fingertips dug into his skin.

'I *probably* won't drop you,' he amended with an apologetic grin.

She looked horrified, but then gave him a slow smile.

For a moment he just stood, delighted by the strange magic of the situation. A mermaid smiling in his arms and the wind singing in his ears.

Then there was a shout in the distance. Sylvain felt a jolt of fear as Neela stiffened in his embrace. In the distance were two men. He saw one wave. He had no idea what they wanted, whether they were hailing them from curiosity, or warning them of the tide, or whether they could see that Sylvain was holding a mermaid. What might such men do with a creature like Neela? Would they put her on show for profit? Cut her apart to sell her scales? Or murder her, blind with terror and hatred of magical creatures?

Sylvain had no intention of finding out.

Fear gave him more strength, though his ill-nourished body trembled with the exertion. Neela clung to him as he waded and clambered over the black and jagged landscape towards the sea. The tide was turning and the further they went, the deeper the pools became, until Neela's hands fluttered against his shoulders.

'This is enough. This is far enough, Sylvain. You must leave me now. For your own safety. I can make it from here alone.'

'Are you sure?' He let his legs collapse beneath him, sinking them both into waist high water, catching his breath.

'I am sure. You have to go back.'

'You are *sure* you will be safe now?'

She smiled into his eyes and then slid more completely into his embrace.

'Thank you.' Neela released him, and with a swirl of her tail she left his arms empty.

She circled him, unpinning her hair and shaking it free.

'You are so lovely,' he said, then blushed as she laughed at him.

Her tail stirred the water so powerfully that he lost his balance. She drew close again and he felt a flash of fear. They were in her element now. Her fangs only flashed a grin.

'My eternal gratitude, Sylvain. And a gift. And my promise.'

He felt something hard and sharp against his palm and drew his hand back swiftly.

'It is only my comb.' Neela held it out to him. 'The comb from my hair.'

'But it's *gold*! I couldn't possibly–'

'Take it. Should you need me, comb the water. Once, twice and thrice, and I will come to you.' Her cool hand touched his cheek gently. 'But now you *must* go back. The sea is rising.'

Sylvain held the comb in his hand, a fortune of pearls and gold, and stared at her.

'Go!' She turned and dipped under the water. With a flick of her tail, she arched and glittered. He watched her swim away, the diamond droplets flung by the sunset fan of her tail. Then he turned and began to wade back towards the shore. A forest of black stone and surging sea separated him from safety. Water poured and swirled, sometimes he had to plunge chest deep. His knees became bruised where the wet rocks were as slippery as ice. He stopped only once to turn and search for sight of her. Currents dragged at him as he clambered and swam.

He staggered at last on shaky legs from the grip of the rising waves. He laughed to see his tangled shirt had washed up amongst the seaweed, the round green bulge of a single apple still trapped within the worn linen.

Sylvain found work aboard the ships eventually, taking whatever jobs he could, provided they never carried him too far from the islands. Short journeys, learning as he went, becoming swift in the rigging, loading and learning to sail. Earning enough to keep his mother well fed, until she passed away. He could afford a new pair of boots and decent shirts for his back. Enough to get by.

Sometimes work was scarce. In the lean times he would take out the mermaid's comb and consider what it was worth. Yet no matter how he had to barter and beg, no matter how poor the pay or how backbreaking the labour, he could not bring himself to part with it. He kept it always in the left inside pocket of his jacket. Jammed deep where the teeth of the comb were forced through the stitching, holding it in place. In high winds and rough storms when he was at sea, he touched his fingers to where it rested near his heart to check that it was safe. When his life seemed bleak and filled with drudgery, he would take it out and examine it. It was proof of magic, a reminder that there was someone wild and beautiful in the world.

He never worked fishing vessels. There was something awful to him in the thrashing glitter of dying fish, their heaving gills and gasping mouths. It made him fear that one day his mermaid might be caught, tangled and terrified, hauled onto filthy, stinking decks. The idea of what could happen to her in the hands of greedy or desperate men troubled him.

He never told a soul what had happened to him. He feared his memories would be reduced by the sharing of them, if they were disbelieved or mocked. He did not speak of her in dark drunken taverns, or laying cramped in the holds of ships amongst brute men, or shivering on decks in screaming winds that tore the tears from the eyes of sailors until they all seemed to weep for their harsh existence.

He never spoke of her at all.

He crewed a ship to England, then found better payment sailing out of Portsmouth on a French vessel bound for Boulogne. The weather darkened, but Sylvain was impatient to head home. He found a berth on a light vessel with mixed cargo heading down the French coast to Cherbourg, then bartered a working passage on a boat headed for Guernsey. He helped drag a heavy, clinking cargo of wooden boxes aboard before the boat sailed at dawn.

The air was sharp. They made excellent speed, with the wind in their favour, except that it blustered and gusted. It would be roaring into their sails one minute, then dropping to whisper around the rigging, before slamming into them again with enough force to take the footing out from under a well-seasoned sailor. The crew tied ropes around their waists, wary of being tossed overboard.

The sea surged and the prow, lifting on the wind, would slap down and shudder, jerking like a cart over rough ground. For more than two hours, Sylvain clung to wet rope and wet wood, watching the waves rise higher in the unsettled sea. The sky remained cloudless, but the wind was wilder now. For the first time in years, Sylvain felt queasy.

A huge wave rolled beneath them, and the boat seemed weightless for a heartbeat. Then it landed with such force that Sylvain's knees struck the deck. His hand slipped on the wet wood as the deck tilted.

The rope around his waist went taut, then snapped. The boat lifted again and Sylvain was thrown into the air. When he fell, he was swallowed whole by the sea.

In the shock of the icy plunge, the shrieking wind was suddenly replaced with the quiet roar of water in his ears. The world was green and still and freezing cold. He kicked and fought his way to the surface, bursting with gasping breaths back into the scream of wind. He flailed, trying to find the boat. It was high above him on the peak of a wave, and it seemed so likely to fall and crush him that Sylvain covered his face with his arms. The sea surged and lifted him so that he was close enough to reach out, fingertips brushing the wood of the hull. Then the sail snapped full in the wind and the boat reared away.

Sylvain bellowed for help, his voice cut off by a slap of water and he coughed, then struck out with strong strokes, for he was an excellent swimmer. The ocean heaved and the boat was lost from view.

'Please!' His voice seemed high and raw in his own ears, like a frightened boy.

The roar of white water thundered, and waves were rolling him, forcing him under into white spinning silence only to leave him again in their whispering wake. It happened again, then again. Each time he fought his way back to the surface. Sometimes there was barely time to suck in a lungful of air before he was trapped in the roiling troughs of great dark waves, a repetitive lurching drop, then a rise as he was pushed skyward, only to be pulled down again.

Another wave began to break high above him and he was dragged into its shadow as it reared. The light shining through the water looked like delicate green glass shattering as it curved and then collapsed on him with a roar like a mountain crumbling. Sylvain spun; his limbs flailed out of his control. It was rough as an avalanche. He kept his eyes squeezed shut.

He broke the surface, coughed and sobbed in air. He was lifted on a cresting wave and then dropped into its glittering wake. His boots were gone, he realised. He reached for his jacket pocket, feeling a sudden panic that the Mermaid's comb would have washed away, and remembered her promise. His chest almost burst with desperate hope. The comb still jutted in the tight confines of his pocket, but he suffered another churning wave before daring to take it out. His fingers were numb. He gripped it so tightly that its sharp edges made his cold fingers bleed.

He combed the water once as the sea swept him down into a dark curling valley between two waves. He combed the water a second time as a mountain of water rose high above him, and as he lifted his hand to stroke the water a third time, a wall of white water struck him from behind like a rockslide. In the instant of impact, the Mermaid's comb was gone from his trembling and bleeding fingers. He clutched hopelessly for it then dove and kicked down, and down … and then it was gone from sight.

The air was aching in his chest. There was silence beneath the surface of the water. A moment of bitter peace in the acceptance of defeat. He looked up, and the surface was a cathedral of moving light as he kicked wearily back towards it. The ocean roared as he burst once more into the air, gasping for breath.

A cloud moved across the sun and the sea turned grey as purgatory. His arms and legs paddled weakly. He choked and fought as he was pulled back under by the current.

Then he was lifted.

Arms were holding him, raising him against the whim of the sea, and as he opened his eyes, he was riding white water at the speed of the breaking waves. Feeling for the hands that were clasped around his chest, he found the mermaid's cold fingers with his own, disbelieving until he saw the delicate frills of the fins that gilded her forearms.

'You came,' he croaked.

She slowed and turned him, so that they were facing. Her eyes were narrowed so coldly he thought she might bite him.

'Of *course* I came,' she almost shouted, 'Did I not say that I would come? Did I not give you my most *precious* possession so that…' She broke off, and her expression softened, as he coughed again and shivered against her violently, his teeth chattering.

'Human, why are you so far from land?' she asked, her head cocked to one side so that her wet hair fell across her high cheekbone.

'I fell off a boat,' Sylvain said, too exhausted to feel humiliated.

Neela tossed her wet hair from her face and blinked. 'Why would you get on a boat when you could ask a mermaid for passage across the sea?' she demanded. 'Did you not want to see me again?'

'Of course I hoped to see you again!' Sylvain said. He tilted his head back a little to look her in the eyes. 'You are the most magical and beautiful thing that I have ever seen.'

'Yet you never used the comb. It has been so long, Sylvain,' Neela's voice was reproachful.

'I'm sorry,' Sylvain shook his head. 'I was scared, and young and stupid. You were like a dream, and I was afraid you would not come. Then all hope of magic and joy and love would be lost forever. And,' he added, 'I was a bit scared that you might eat me.'

'*Eat* you?' She stared at him, lips slightly parted in disbelief. Her limpid gaze so close and lovely it made his heart race. Then she gurgled with laughter.

'I'm sorry, I'm sorry, forgive me for waiting so long, Neela!'

He embraced her as tightly as his weak arms would allow, and let his head fall against her neck. There was only the suggestion of warmth from her cool body, but he clung to her, his teeth chattering, shivering so hard he thought she would surely complain.

Rain began to lash down, but they rode the storm homewards. They slipped past white water and swooped through the deep troughs between waves with such delicious speed that Sylvain felt an exhilaration he had not known since he was a child. They rode the waves to shore, Neela catching the white water, spinning him slowly. She carried him as he had carried her, weightless and elegant in her element, cresting waves in a slow waltz. Cold and exhausted as he was, when he saw land, his stomach clenched in disappointment rather than relief.

'I wish we could do this forever,' he whispered. 'I lost your comb, but I could not bear it if I didn't see you again.'

'Sylvain you could have seen me any time these past years,' Neela said. 'And now you have thrown my comb into the sea. I cannot simply linger in the shallows for the next few years until you remember me again.'

'No, of course not! Please, forgive me, you have always been in my heart. I never married,' he blurted before he realised that her eyes were dancing with laughter again.

He asked haltingly, 'Are you...? Do your people *marry*? Is it too late for us, or-?'

She threw back her head, and laughed at him, then kissed him as they whirled at the crest of a wave.

Sylvain was considered by many to have suddenly grown very eccentric for such a young man. He moved into an ancient, abandoned fisherman's cottage so close to the water that it was known to flood during the spring tides. He made a comfortable living trading in things he claimed to have found in the sea.

Local women tried to catch the attention of this handsome, carefree bachelor in vain. He was often absent from the island, claiming to be 'trading', although he neither owned a boat, nor ever seemed to book passage on one.

He was odd in other ways too. Even in the dead of winter he had been seen swimming further out to sea than could be considered safe. Some of the locals shook their heads at the mention of his name. A well-known gossip, who occasionally took the time to pry near to Sylvain's ramshackle little house, returned to town one day to say that she had quite distinctly seen two people swimming in the distance. Their heads were close together in the sparkling, sunlit sea, and the sound of laughter rang out over the crashing of the waves.

BLACK DOGS

'It seems to leave the darkness rather blacker than before ...'

Sir Arthur Conan Doyle

'I wouldn't do that if I was you.'

Paul turned, hand on the door, uncertain if it was him that was being addressed.

'I'm sorry?'

'I wouldn't go out there if I was you.'

A man in a rough hemp shirt was tamping tobacco into a short pipe. He sat at the table closest to the fire, silhouetted by the glow, and gestured at the door with the pipe.

'But,' Paul glanced at the woman behind the bar who was polishing a pewter tankard. 'Isn't it closing time?'

'You didn't hear the howling?' she asked.

'Dog,' said a smartly dressed older man, sat at the end of the bar.

'I didn't hear anything,' Paul glanced back to the man by the fire. 'I'm sure–'

'No, lad. A *Black Dog*.' The man raised his pipe above his head to indicate height.

'*Big* one,' said the woman behind the bar.

The man swept his arm out to point the pipe at the bartender. 'And there, Mary has struck to the heart of the matter. The dog, lad, is *big*.'

He smiled, tapped his pipe briefly against his own chest, and said, 'My name's Kemp. You'd better sit awhile until this is past.'

He nudged the chair next to him with his foot so that it scraped across the floor and tilted precariously before settling with a bang.

'Until... a *dog* is past?' Paul smiled. 'Thank you for the offer, Mr Kemp. But if it's all the same–'

'Englishman,' said the man at the bar, shaking his head in slow disapproval.

Paul frowned. 'Yes, I am English, as it happens – and in England we don't hide inside just because there's a dog.'

'This is a big one,' said the bartender.

Paul saw the pipe jab back towards the bar. 'Once again, Mary has it in a nutshell. It is a dog of unusual size. What's your name, young man?'

'It's Paul. Look, thank you, but–'

'It's huge,' interrupted the man at the bar.

Paul laughed. 'Huge? Exactly how big do dogs get in Guernsey that people hide inside?'

'If you'll sit awhile, I can tell you,' Kemp's pipe was pointed meaningfully at the chair beside him, but Paul held up his hands to decline.

'Thanks all the same, but two's my limit. I'm low on money and I have an early sailing tomorrow, so I will bid you goodnight, Mr Kemp.'

Mary banged the tankard on the bar. 'A drink on the house then!' she snapped, and winced as though the words had injured her.

'Generous of you, Mary,' the man at the bar commented, pushing forward his tankard.

'Not for you, you old Jersey skinflint!'

Before Paul could refuse again, the door flew open, and a woman entered in a swirl of dress and shawl. Paul had to step back to avoid a collision. The woman was young and dishevelled. She slammed the door and shot the bolt, before leaning her back against it with her eyes closed.

'Dog!' she said, between gasping breaths.

'We're not deaf, Nelia,' said the man with the pipe.

'*He* is apparently,' remarked the man at the bar, tilting his chin at Paul.

'Don't be rude, Gabbon,' said Mary, beginning to fill the tankard. 'What are you having, Nelia?'

'To calm *me* down right now? Two of everything maybe?' The young woman was still trying to catch her breath. She noticed Paul, and smiled. 'Hello, you're new.'

'Hello, Miss Nelia. I'm Paul. Can I... *May* I buy you a drink?'

'Oh *now* he can afford a drink.' Mary threw up a dismissive hand and grabbed a bottle from the shelf. 'Have a Brandy, Nelia. You're white as a ghost. You, what's your name? Paul? Get her by the fire.'

Kemp stood to pull over another chair, and Nelia waved the men off as they both tried to help her into a seat.

'I'm scared, gentlemen, and out of breath, not ill. Thank you, Mary. Goodness, my hands are shaking so much!'

'Did you see it?' Kemp demanded. 'Which one was it?'

'How should I know?' Nelia sipped at her brandy and winced at the taste. 'I ran half the way here with my hands over my eyes. I'm surprised I didn't fall in the harbour! I was taking an apple pie to Mrs Ogier, but she wasn't in. So there I was, half a mile from home with nowhere to hide. It couldn't have happened at a worse time.'

'Where's the pie?' Gabbon asked curiously, turning on his barstool.

'Oh I threw it.' Nelia sat back and dismissed the lost pie with a wave of her hand.

'You threw a pie at a dog?' Paul asked. 'Why?'

Nelia tilted her head and looked at him. 'You're not from here, are you?'

A howl, distant and low, rose and fell in the night outside. It was unmistakably made by something very large.

The tavern fell silent except for the cracking and popping of wood in the fire.

'I bet dogs like pies,' Gabbon said, turning back to the bar.

The deep, low howling kept them all trapped in the tavern.

Paul, unsettled, drank more than he usually would have, and tried to follow the conversation unfolding about the Black Dogs of Guernsey. Mary had built up the fire, and they were all now seated around the closest table, which was cluttered with bottles and glasses.

'So, there are seven?' Paul asked, holding up six fingers and then wrinkling his nose in confusion.

'No,' Kemp said firmly.

Paul looked at his hands and then rubbed his eyes with them. 'I'm confused,' he said. 'If even *seeing* one of these things kills you, how is anybody managing to count? How can you tell the difference?'

'Exactly!' Nelia said. 'But they do all have distinct territories. They don't all *kill* you either… at least, not right away.'

'I reckon there's five,' Mary said, and gave a sharp nod as though the matter was settled.

'Five in all of the Channel Islands?' Paul asked.

'Good grief, no,' Mary chuckled. 'Bless your heart. Five in Guernsey.'

'Is that counting the old dog or not?' Kemp asked.

'Why would I count the old dog? He's in Sark! No. Five dogs *not* counting the old dog.'

'So wait, there's a dog in Sark now?' Paul demanded.

'There's always been dog in Sark. Keep up, lad.' Kemp winked at him.

'The Old Dog of the Coupée.' Mary swept a hand out dramatically. 'For as long as anyone remembers, the old dog has walked the long track at night. Some people believe that if he walks alongside you, it is an omen of death. If not *your* death, then the death of somebody in your family.'

'So if you have a rich aunt, in her nineties, it's not much to worry about.' Kemp shrugged. 'It would probably still be enough to scare you daft, mind you.'

'I thought the Sark dog was white,' Gabbon said.

'What?'

'The old dog in Sark. I thought that one was *white*.'

'A giant white dog? Whoever heard of a giant white dog? Where did you hear that rubbish?' Kemp chuckled.

'Jersey,' Mary pursed her lips and shook her head. 'Jersey people are always getting things muddled in their heads.'

Gabbon opened his mouth to argue, but caught the wicked gleam in Mary's eye and coughed out a laugh. 'Pass me that bottle, you awful woman. *Our* dog in Jersey, the Black Dog of Bouley Bay – now he's a *good* one.' Gabbon gave a satisfied nod as though he had trained the dog himself. 'The Bouley Bay dog is a storm herald. He howls so loud he can be heard all along the North coast. A mournful wail that chills the blood. A sound that hangs over you like the shroud of death, letting you know that your end is near if you set out to sea. And he's big as a bull. The biggest of them all!'

'Good grief! That's the most words I've heard you say since the time you thought I'd over-charged you for that whisky!' Mary said, a smile lightened her hard expression for a moment. 'And how would you know he's the biggest? Been out and measured them all, have you?' She gave him a wink.

Gabbon smiled awkwardly and shuffled in his seat. He took a moment straightening the handkerchief in his top pocket and cleared his throat. 'Of course, these days people think the Bouley Bay dog is a monster. Burning eyes, breathing fire, dragging chains and murdering people up and down the coast. But those are just rumours spread by the smugglers. None of it's true, he's a very good dog. When the smugglers want people to stay inside, they kick up a racket, howling and clanking chains. Then, when everybody has scurried home safe, they can carry all their booze off the ships without having to worry about being seen. They've been doing it for years. They do it here too, of course.'

'So wait, wait, hang on!' Paul sat back in his chair, holding up his hands. 'If there are smugglers pretending to be giant dogs... And if you *know* there are smugglers pretending to be giant dogs, with the howling, and the frightening everybody, then...' he pointed to the window. 'How do you know that's a *real* dog? How do you know that *any* of the dogs are real for that matter? It's a great story, isn't it? There's a giant black dog, but you can't check if it's real because if you look at it, or it looks at you, then you'll die! How convenient for the smugglers that there's a monster nobody can look at. How can we know that it isn't *all* made up nonsense?'

Nelia shrugged. 'I have some friends who bring in a few bottles from France now and then. They've got this sort of costume, like a blanket they throw over themselves with ears sewn on and a long tail, in case they get seen by the excise men. It gets the job done at night. My friend David, he's the dog's arse.'

'So then,' Paul spread his hands, and then slapped them down on the table. 'If you know it's just smugglers making it all up, why are we hiding in here? I'm supposed to sail at dawn!'

'That's a shame,' Nelia said softly.

He turned to her, blinking.

'How do we know there are *real* black dogs?' Kemp shook out a match and drew on his pipe slowly, making sure he had Paul's attention again before answering. 'We know because of the dead people, Paul.'

'Dead people? But... what if that's just smugglers covering their tracks? If they run into some poor soul and they...' He trailed off as he noticed that everybody else around their table was shaking their head.

'No man could ever kill somebody the way those people died.' Kemp refilled his glass.

Mary passed a hand over her eyes. 'The people who see the Grim...' she paused, took a sip from her cup. 'The fear on them, what it does to them ... it's like a sickness.'

'What if it's the fear itself that finishes them off? And the other one... what did you call it?'

'The Barghast,' she said quietly.

Paul listed them off on his fingers. 'So that's a grim, a barghast, a hellhound, a tower dog… That's only four?'

'The locals swear that there are two grims – one with chains, and one without, and they each stick to their territories.'

Paul laid his hands flat on the table. 'Right, let's start again, please. How many giant black dogs are there in Guernsey?'

Kemp held up a single finger. 'So first there's the Black Dog of Rue de la Bete…'

'It means *"road of the beast"*,' Nelia interjected helpfully.

Kemp nodded. 'There used to be a prison there, full of the most evil men imaginable. Ship-wreckers and murderers and… well, you know…'

'Yes but it's not *that* lane called Rue de la Bete where the black dog turns up,' Mary argued. 'There's another one near L'Eree. That's where the dog they call The Beast roams after dark. Now, that one is *definitely* a grim. A grim is the type of black dog that shows itself to people who are doomed to die. Do you remember when it happened to old what's-his-name?'

'Vaucourt?' Kemp nodded at Mary. 'Yes I remember that. Didn't the damn thing jump into his cart when he was driving home and scare him to death?'

'No, that one only appears to people who are marked for death. Old Vaucourt died the *next* day. So it must have been a grim. Stands to reason. If it hadn't been a grim, Vaucourt would have keeled over on the spot.'

'No hold on, hold on, that can't be right. I thought the grim was the dog that roams by the old slaughterhouse at Clos du Valle, the one called *Lé Chien Bodu*?' Kemp sat back squinting as he tried to remember.

'That's right!' Nelia bounced up and down in her chair and flapped a hand. 'I've heard of that one! See, I think either there's more than one grim, or there's a grim that goes wherever it chooses to on the island, showing itself to those who are marked for death and so they already have the scent of the sepulchre upon them.'

'Scent of the *sepulchre* upon them? Where did you get that fancy word? What are you, French?' Kemp grinned at her.

Nelia laughed and kicked Kemp under the table.

'So hang on…' Paul interrupted. 'Which one is the hellhound then?'

'That would be the red-eyed dog of the manor,' Gabbon said. 'Only one person ever caught a glimpse of that one and lived to tell of it, so they say.'

'Lived! Ha! If you can call it *living* when a man only survives to scream himself insane in an attic for six months and then throws himself off the roof.' Kemp glanced at Mary.

'Bad business that,' she said. 'Trevor it was – a cousin of mine. Mad as a hedge after he saw that bloody dog.' Mary frowned. 'He described it, while he was still screaming mind you… saying the Dog had flaming eyes, flaming breath and that it was so hideous of aspect–'

'*Hideous of aspect?*' Nelia exclaimed. 'Who sounds all fancy French now?'

'So that one's called a *hellhound*? Because of its flaming eyes?' Paul asked.

'It's actually called *La Bete de la Devise de Saumarez a Saint Martin*, but that's a bit of a mouthful when you're trying to warn people to run away.' Kemp waved his pipe at Paul. 'Better just to shout *"hellhound!"* More succinct, gets your point across faster, and it saves you some air in your lungs for running.'

'They found giant paw prints scorched in the ground when it killed Trevor's friend. Trevor kept screaming something about it opening its mouth as it lunged, and hellfire roaring out and burning his friend as it savaged him.' Mary shuddered.

'So… was his friend's body burned, or did he just die of fright, or…?' Paul was curious.

'Eaten,' Kemp nodded. 'They found one of his boots all scorched though.'

'Trevor said that boy was eaten alive,' Mary said. 'Screaming his sins. Although in the end, Trevor was just screaming about screaming. Very unsettling watching a man scream like that. His eyebrows were all scorched off as well. Made him look surprised. Wish I hadn't visited to be honest, although it seemed like the right thing to do at the time. I never did like Trevor. Or his brother Christian.' Mary narrowed her eyes. 'I'm glad Christian moved to Jersey. Something about those two brothers always put my teeth on edge.' She shuddered and took a drink.

'I heard that hellhounds only come for the worst sort of people. I didn't like to say, what with him being your cousin and all, but if he was friends with that other lad, the one that got eaten...' Kemp shrugged awkwardly. 'He was a nasty piece of work, that lad that got eaten.'

Paul looked around curiously as everyone else at the table exchanged knowing glances.

There was a pause and then Nelia said, 'I though it was the tower dog that had burning eyes. Isn't it the tower dog that's a barghast?'

'Different sort of burning, with that one.' Kemp nodded sagely. 'The Tower Dog's eyes are said to burn with *blue* flames.'

'It's a cold burn.' Mary glanced at the fire. 'He likes the cold, the Tower Dog. Usually only comes in Winter. Near Christmas.'

'Especially near the Winter solstice. A soul eater, looking for a hot meal.' Gabbon rubbed his hands together briskly and blew on them as though he was suddenly feeling the cold more acutely.

Mary stood quietly and put another log on the fire.

'*Soul eater?*' Paul shivered and pulled his jacket tighter. 'It is rather unseasonably cold, isn't it?'

He looked around from face to face, noticing the fear that lined each expression. 'I can see why you got scared and threw that pie then, Nelia.'

They exchanged smiles.

'Right then. So, not counting the black – *or possibly white* – dog in Sark, or the Black Dog in Jersey–'

'There's two in Jersey,' interjected Gabbon. 'Not including the one in St Peter's Valley, because that's the ghost of a normal dog, so he doesn't count, otherwise there'd be three.'

'*Two* is there now?' Mary said sitting back down. 'Well I suppose that's slightly less embarrassing than only having *one* giant black dog on your whole island. What's this other one? I suppose that one's as big as a bull as well, is it?'

'I'm not too sure about the other one, actually.' Gabbon looked thoughtful. 'Very old legend. Mostly forgotten stories of a giant black dog in Petit Port, with broken gold chains, who guards a–'

'Oh *gold* chains is it? *Gold?* Iron chains aren't good enough for a Jersey dog I suppose?' Mary grinned at Gabbon, and he smiled.

'I'm just telling you what I heard, Mary.'

'What does it guard?' Nelia asked, her large eyes wide with curiosity.

'Not sure, actually. Depends on the version. Ancient treasure, some say, or a passage to hell, or a door to the underworld, or the land of the fée.'

'Why would you need to *guard* a door to hell?' Mary asked throwing her hands in the air. 'Who's trying to sneak into hell, if I may be so bold as to ask? Although you Jersey folk are so wicked it probably saves time to have a short-cut.'

This time Mary got a hearty laugh out of Gabbon before he continued. 'Probably it's a fée legend. All those old legends got mixed up with religious concerns when the church got involved in calling *les fée* "unchristian" and pretending you could scare anything off with a crucifix.'

'What are these fée then?' Paul began to ask, but Nelia made a sharp gesture with her hand.

'Don't start with the faeries! It's too much! My mother had a terrible experience with a faery when she moved here from Madeira.'

'Speaking of Madeira...' Gabbon sat up cheerfully. 'Didn't you have a bottle of that good Madeira wine left from last Christmas, Mary?'

Paul closed his eyes as Mary got up, and then he started counting again. 'So *not* including the dogs in Sark or Jersey...'

'Or Alderney,' Kemp interrupted before taking a swig.

'There's a Black Dog in Alderney?'

'Not a clue. They do have problems with selkies though.'

Paul patiently exhaled. 'So not including *any* of the other islands, there's probably what, two grims, a hellhound and the tower dog, is that right?'

'At least,' said Kemp, pulling his pipe out again.

Another howl cut through the night and they all listened until it faded away, exchanging glances at how close it sounded.

'And then of course, there's that headless dog,' Mary said, returning from the bar and continuing the conversation.

'There's *what*?' Paul turned in his seat to look at her.

'We're not including the headless dog of Le Ville au Roi,' Kemp said firmly. 'Because he's a *ghost*, so he doesn't count.'

'He is big though, and black, so maybe he should count.' Mary set the bottle of Madeira wine in front of Gabbon.

'Can't count a dog with no head,' said Kemp tapping his pipe on the table. 'It's not even a whole dog for a start. Besides, it never hurt anybody.'

'Well that's not strictly true.' Nelia tilted her head. 'My friend David, who I told you about, you know, the dog's backside? He and his brother ran into it one night after drinking half a bottle of rum, and it scared them daft. David said he swung for it with the bottle, but the dog had no substance, so the bottle passed right through it.' Nelia waved her hand in a circle. 'So he spun right round, lost his footing, and fell in the ditch. Gave his ankle a nasty sprain. His brother had to give him a piggy-back home. Neither of them can hold their drink though, so it might just have been a normal dog.'

'This David,' Paul asked nonchalantly. 'Is he your sweetheart, or...?'

Nelia looked at him, then snorted with laughter.

'*So*,' Mary said. 'We have at least five and seven-eighths worth of black dogs if you count the headless dog of La Ville au Roi.'

'Which we definitely do *not!*' Kemp set his pipe down on the table and he and Mary glared at each other.

'I don't know,' said Gabbon. 'I don't think hellhounds and barghasts are different things. Besides there's shape-shifters in the islands so...'

Paul slumped in his chair.

'Sorry, lad,' Gabbon said.

'Really I just want to know what sort of dog is most likely to be outside,' Paul said, sloshing a little more rum into his tankard.

'Here? This close, in the town?' Mary sighed. 'Oh bless your heart, lad, it'll be the Tower Dog. The soul eater. This is his territory, and everybody knows to stay inside when you hear him howl.'

They fell silent, then Paul sat up sharply, listening. A moment later Kemp set his pipe down as he heard it too. There was the distinct sound of metal scraping against stone. Paul realised he was hearing the clattering of heavy chains being pulled over cobbles. He opened his mouth to speak, and a deafening howl began. First low and mournful, then eerily high. It fell away in volume and then rumbled into a loud growl, which seemed to shake the table.

They all stood, chairs scraping back, tense and terrified. Poised to flee, although there was nowhere to run. Frost crackled as it lined the windows. White snowy flowers bloomed across the tiny leaded panes, turning them to white lace. Beyond their veiled opacity, the light of the lanterns outside dimmed to black as something blocked first one window, and then the next.

The fire in the grate turned to sapphire flames that licked close against the wood, as though cowering from the cold. The candle-flames shrank and turned pale.

'Heavens defend us,' whispered Mary.

Paul felt suddenly terribly cold, like a December wind had cut through his clothes and put an ache in his chest. A weight seemed to press down on him. All the weariness of long days at sea and the despair of sleepless nights. It was an effort to inhale the bitter air.

Nelia's fingers brushed his hand and he clasped at her like a drowning man. She hugged him, sudden and fierce, her face against his neck, and he could feel her shaking as he held her close. He knew he was as scared as she was, but hoped, at least, that his body blocked the cutting cold for her in the way that hers did for him.

The sound of rough breathing and the dragging of chains stopped at the door, and Paul felt the alcohol in his stomach turn to ice-water. There was snuffling, great lungs huffing and exhaling air. The noises of a giant black dog sniffing for something. Everyone in the bar was silent. Paul wondered if the others were all holding their breath as well.

The door jumped against its hinges, with a bang and a scrape, and they all trembled and clutched at each other. The sound was repeated with more force. Paul pictured the huge paw striking at the door as it rattled again, imagining claws as long as his fingers. Then there was a crash of chains as the dog threw its weight against the thick wood, a battering of clawing and scratching. A growl sounded like rocks grating in the walls, drowning out all other sound.

Kemp pushed past Paul, startling him from his frozen terror.

'Get the table,' Kemp said.

Nelia stepped away, jumping to help the older man. The three of them knocked over a great oak table. It landed on its side with a crash, and Paul threw his shoulder to the task with Kemp, pushing it up against the door as the scratching and clawing and growling from outside grew more ferocious.

The heavy wooden door, shuddering and slamming against the frame, was bowing in the centre. The thick planks seemed suddenly flimsy to Paul's mind. As he stared, a pale patch of frost blossomed in the centre of the door. He saw little splinters crack away under the crushing force of another blow. Paul remembered tales of ships' hulls becoming brittle and cracking under the force of Arctic ice, and realised the door might be even weaker than he had thought.

'It's going to get in,' he said, surprised that his voice sounded calm.

Claws broke through a crack in the frozen door, scattering chunks of icy wood, which slid across the floor.

'Mary!' Gabbon suddenly held out an imperious arm. 'Pass me that horrible single malt whisky that near melted my teeth.'

'You said it wasn't fit to disinfect a wound.'

'I know.'

Mary hesitated. 'There's others nearly as strong, and that taste a lot better. That one's a poor choice for a final drink.'

'I'm not going to drink it, Love. Hand it over, *please*.'

Gabbon took it and pulled the cork out with his teeth. He plucked his handkerchief from his pocket and jammed it into the neck of the bottle. 'Match please, Kemp.' He held out a hand.

Kemp struck a flaring match that shrunk to a tiny blue bud. Gabbon shook the bottle once and lit the handkerchief. For a moment Paul thought the cloth wouldn't catch, but then the fine cotton began to blacken and flare with blue light.

A plank of wood snapped by the handle, and a freezing gust of white blossomed through the gap. Gabbon gritted his teeth and stepped forward. He leant towards the hole in the door and shoved the bottle past the frozen splinters. With a lash of his arm, he hurled the whisky bottle down hard. There was a smash and a *whump* as the alcohol caught fire.

Gabbon recoiled, cradling his hand, which was white with frost. Outside the door there was the raw sound of a deep yelp turned to furious growling and snarling. There was snapping of jaws and then more deep yelping that retreated up the street, chains dragging with rattling speed. Nelia was furiously wiping frost from one of the little windowpanes and trying to see through.

'I think its tail is smoking!' She laughed a little wildly, then sat down abruptly on the floor, breathing hard, with her hand to her chest.

'Well done.' Paul went to shake Gabbon's hand, realised the man was hurt, and settled for squeezing his shoulder.

Mary pulled off her shawl to wrap about Gabbon's arm, pulling him closer to the fire. The flames roared once more in the grate, turning orange, and the air in the room became less frigid.

'You daft old fool! You're lucky you didn't just set the door on fire,' Mary scolded. 'You could have gotten your hand bitten clean off. That dog could have had a drink and a snack in one mouthful. Nelia! Make sure this place isn't about to catch fire, will you? There's a bucket of water in the kitchen.'

'It was here for *me*, that Dog. I can feel it.' Gabbon was staring at the floor.

'It might well have wanted to kill us all. What makes you so special?' Mary asked.

'I don't know. I could feel the eyes of the thing looking for me, even through the door. Like the north wind blowing through me. My life ripping from my bones.'

'Well, it didn't sodding get you, did it?' Mary said. 'Here you sit, threatening to die while owing me at least three shillings! And having vanquished a monster like the knights of old, you're planning to lay down and push up daisies? What use was all that heroism and keeping the damn dog out if you're just going to sit there and scare yourself into a heart attack now it's gone?'

'Mary...'

'It's true,' Nelia said getting up. 'What if it's like what we were saying? That half the time it's *believing* you'll die that makes you die?'

'I just...' Gabbon shook his head.

'Right then.' Mary stamped around behind the bar, took down a bottle and slammed it down with enough force to make them all jump. 'Here's your choice. Sit there like a great lump and scare yourself to death, or...'

'Or? I know that's your best brandy, Mary love, but–'

'Or drink free every night for a week until this dying nonsense is out of your head.'

'What Jersey man wouldn't fend off death for free drinks?' Kemp asked, sinking into a chair.

'And...' Mary set down two glasses, leant forward over the bar and eyed Gabbon with a hostile gaze. 'You marry me in April, get your lazy backside on the other side of this bar, and do some work for a change.'

Gabbon stared hard at the bottle. His face had regained some colour. 'I'm in here most of the time anyway, I suppose,' he said.

'I had noticed.'

Paul felt Nelia's hand squeeze his and they exchanged smiles.

Gabbon carefully poured out two splashes of brandy with his uninjured hand, raised his glass, and glared back at Mary. 'Here's to you then, Mrs Gabbon!'

'I'll be keeping my own name, thank you very much,' she snapped. 'And don't imagine I shall be forgetting about the three shillings either.'

They toasted.

L'ÊMÂNUE

Your curious hand grips the fruit but it doesn't pull away from the tree. You are lifted into the air. You try to let go, but your fingers have sunk deep into the sweet flesh. You feel the hot pit on your fingertips. Branches coil around your body as you are drawn into the trunk.

Tin Doom

There are certain woodland areas on the islands where it is inadvisable to walk alone. As far back as can be remembered, there are rumours of an 'invisible beast'; a thing more sensed than seen that lurks in the trees. Sometimes there is an unsettling movement, or whispering of the leaves when the wind is not blowing, or a sudden glimpse of blazing golden eyes.

Although unseen, *L'Êmânue* was suspected to be responsible for the disappearance of people over a period of many long years. Those missing had entered old forest land. They were never seen again, except that sometimes, years or even decades later, a pile of bones would be discovered at the foot of a tree. The bones were always white and clean, gleaming as though polished, but had multiple fractures marring their pale surface.

One lost boy from a wealthy family, whose bones were not found for almost twenty years, was only identified when his ageing mother recognised the small, golden Saint Christopher necklace that she had given him. It was still wound about the fragile bones of his neck.

For generations, young children were warned not to venture into the woods alone or after dark, as is only common sense. Most children who disobeyed were punished by nothing more severe than stern words from disappointed parents. But occasionally a little boy or girl would take a shortcut through quiet woodland, or go seeking adventure, or play too far from their friends and family. And sometimes, those children would simply disappear. They were never found, no matter how the people of the islands searched for them.

Always, many years later, a small and broken skeleton would be found in the woods.

This left the islanders with a disturbing mystery. The skeleton was always complete, down to the smallest finger-bone, and it was always found beneath a tree with no sign that it had ever been buried or moved. In Alderney, a group of men cut down a stunted elder tree where a young woman's bones had been discovered. They found the tree to be entirely normal. Its wood was wood like any other. It burned as wood is supposed to burn.

In the summer of 1747 in Guernsey, a woodcutter named Le Salle went to cut trees in a small copse of oaks and did not return. When his absence was noticed, searchers saw where he had left his cart, and entered the woods. Only a few steps into the shadows of the trees they found his axe where it had been dropped. It lay next to a huge, old tree that had a single pale cut in its trunk: Le Salle had struck it one solitary blow. There was no other sign or trace of him to be found.

The news spread fear and confusion, and the older generations reminded people of the ancient tales, the stories of missing children, and of people who had seen the flashes of green or golden eyes. They insisted that there was something out there in the woods. Something old and patient, which made the leaves stir when the air was still.

'L'Êmânue,' they whispered.

The invisible beast that stole people away and killed them, and kept their bodies until they were almost forgotten, and then left their bones beneath a tree.

What manner of creature, people asked in hushed tones, could attack and overpower a man of Le Salle's considerable size and strength? A man wielding a heavy axe, no less. What could take him unawares and overpower him so completely that it left no sign of struggle, not even a drop of blood, to suggest that he had been able to fight back? There were no drag marks or tracks or footprints. He was simply gone.

Whoever started the fire that night is unknown, but it burned ferociously in the late summer heat. The flames entirely consumed the copse of trees where La Salle had disappeared. Some of the younger children that lived nearby complained of a thin, high-pitched screaming above the roar of the fire, loud enough to wake them. Since none of the adults in the area heard anything of the sort, it was dismissed as a children's fancy, or a silly lie spread amongst the young people.

In 1886 in Jersey a young French couple and their little daughter were gathering wood for winter in an ancient, overgrown orchard. Jacqueline was keeping an eye on Lydie as they gathered kindling. Leo worked with a hatchet to cut dead wood and small branches to pile in their cart. Leo was finding that their pony, ordinarily a sweet and affectionate creature, was behaving in an ill-tempered and snappish manner, refusing to settle down. After the third time that she persistently dragged the braked cart from where Leo wanted it, he tied her halter to a low branch.

The pony rolled her eyes and stamped, withers shuddering, and Leo patted her side before picking up the hatchet again.

He turned his head at the sound of a sharp scream, the sort of noise his daughter made when she fell and skinned her knee. It was the raw shriek of terror from his wife Jacqueline that set him running. He ducked past low branches, and the whip of brambles, to see his wife clawing at the twisted trunk of a tree. Her fingers were bloody, her nails ragged, she was screaming their daughter's name, over and over.

'Where's Lydie?' he asked in confusion.

Even as the words left his mouth, he saw the tangled and entwined vines around the base of the tree flex and tighten like laces in a boot. Within them he saw his daughter's pale fingertips reaching desperately for her mother, then they too disappeared as she was drawn deeper into the tangle and swallowed entircly.

He struck at the twisted branches, hacking desperately with the hatchet to try and carve her free, terrified lest he should strike her. The hatchet sent chips of bark flying and the blade bit deeper than he had expected into something softer and wetter than wood.

Branches flinched and a vine lashed out. Leo was struck hard enough to lift him from his feet. His world spun, sky and earth flashed across his vision. He hit the ground on his stomach. He struggled to his knees as Jacqueline grabbed the hatchet that had fallen from his hand. She slashed and hacked.

Leo heard an eerie scream so high-pitched that it was barely more than the sound of the wind in the leaves. Vines whipped towards his wife, twigged claws were stretching for her, and just for an instant Leo saw the whole of the monster as it moved. The sheer size of the creature, and the subtle difference of its rough skin against the bark of the tree with which it was intertwined, was now visible.

Its face, which was distorted with fury, loomed above his wife and child. Leo stumbled forward and wrenched at the knotted limbs which held his daughter, his strength born of horror. He glimpsed her blonde hair, and then was struck by the monster again. A blow from a flailing branch on the back of his neck. He heard his wife cry out as a fist of twigs and leaves tangled in her hair. Leo rolled over, and saw it wrench her head back.

The creature twisted down, its green eyes blazing with horrible intelligence.

Leo grabbed the hatchet from Jacqueline's hand. He leapt, striking with desperate fear, and slammed the blade deep into the side of its head. The monster shrieked, a sound like a furious wind tearing through a forest. It released Leo's wife, and then his daughter.

A sudden flailing, an untangling of branches, a rush of dark sap, and his daughter slid free as though reborn. She collapsed at his feet, fighting to breathe, her mouth and nose filled with honey-thick liquid. Jacqueline scrambled to help her, and Leo grabbed them and pulled them both back. The monster, still very much alive, thrashed and struggled to free itself from the tree. Real vines of ivy, thick as a man's wrist, had wound about its multiple, spidery limbs, and lashed it to its surroundings.

The creature must have been wreathed around the tree for decades at least, Leo realised. Silently waiting, patient and hungry, for a victim to step close enough.

A horror hiding in plain sight.

Lydie, her mouth free of sap, drew air deep into her lungs and began screaming as they carried her away.

The monster finally tore loose, spraying earth from false roots and raining leaves and sap. Leo blinked debris from his eyes as he led his family towards the rearing pony and the cart. He was terrified that the monster would pursue them but, as he watched, the creature moved suddenly and with appalling speed away through the branches of the treetops, deeper into the woods.

Leo, Jacqueline and Lydie moved back to France a few weeks later. Lydie still showed some red marks where the strange caustic sap had begun to irritate her skin before her parents could find water to wash it off.

Leo's tale of *L'Êmânue* caused more disbelief than fear in the local population. Many of the islanders had never heard of such a thing. Some people remembered the old legends well enough to put a name to what the French family described, but they only considered *L'Êmânue* a superstitious folk tale.

Despite the scratches and bruises on Jacqueline's face, or perhaps because of them, most people thought Leo a liar when he warned them of the danger hiding in the trees. One old woman from Guernsey waved Leo away and told him impatiently that she was well aware of *L'Êmânue*. Such monsters grew much bigger in Guernsey, she said, and he should be thankful he had not met one of those.

While most people mocked, or swiftly forgot the French family after their departure, others quietly believed them. Once again parents repeated the old stories of the monsters and faery creatures that live in the islands. They warned their children of why it is always wise to stay out of the older woods. They told them to avoid quiet places, where the birds do not sing, but the leaves whisper even when the wind is still.

KELPIES

When the hands of the foam shall beckon and flee.
And the Kelpie riders ride for the sea.

William Bliss Carman

Jenny's patience was wearing thin.

It was getting late, and she was tired after a long day of oversee-ing tomato pickers, hauling boxes, and loading carts on her father's farm. Her father had hired fifteen additional labourers to deal with the larger-than-expected crop of Guernsey tomatoes. He had asked her to show these men to their lodgings, which were a mile or so along the coast. However, after they had finished work, these fifteen men had other ideas and made their way directly to the nearest tavern. They seemed to be doing their best to drink away as much of the money they had earned that day, in as short a time as possible. The tavern was a stop Jenny had not wished to make. Now the men were finally emerging from the bar, reeling drunk and questioning her about how they were going to get to their beds.

The fifteen men consisted of Graham from Scotland, two brothers from Sark, three French men, two cousins from Alderney, an English boy who didn't talk much, four Jersey vraic gatherers, and two grave-diggers, who were grumbling openly about the persistent good health of the Guernsey populace this year.

Two hours in the company of these men had made Jenny wish that her father was more discerning when he hired additional labour, but the harvest had been huge this year. They had made excellent money, but

Jenny suspected they would end up with more tomatoes than they could possibly sell. They would probably end up inviting anyone who wanted to come and pick all the tomatoes they could carry, so that the excess of tomatoes did not rot on the vine. Such generosity was often rewarded by cheerful gifts of their tomatoes returned to them in jars and pots as sauces and soups and chutneys, but managing these fifteen men was making Jenny loathe tomatoes more than she had thought possible.

'It's only a mile along the coast,' she told them patiently, and then answered their questions – *no*, there was no cart they could borrow, everything was full of tomatoes. No, she would not *unload* a cart for them. No, there were no donkeys to carry them. Yes, she knew Guernsey was famous for donkeys, but there were no donkeys closer than Mrs Valois' barn where they were supposed to sleep.

'So,' she said loudly, resisting the urge to scowl, 'it *really* is fastest if we just walk. Now, shall we go?'

She wrinkled her nose in disgust as she noticed one of the vraic gatherers was urinating on the wall of the tavern.

'Right then!' She said clapping her hands. 'Anybody who actually wants to sleep under a roof tonight, let's get moving, or I'll just leave you here and you can sleep in a hedge.'

The tall glass of cider that she'd finished had made her bolder than usual. She started walking and felt relief as she heard the grumbling and sounds of unsteady footsteps behind her. Hopefully she wouldn't leave any stragglers.

The sun was dipping beneath the horizon, turning the sky shades of pink and gold. By the time she led the men to their beds and turned back, she'd be walking home in the darkness. Even at fifteen years old, the thought still unnerved her. There were too many tales and rumours of dangerous monsters that lived in the islands. Black dogs that could kill you with a look. Goblins and glowing lights. Faery men and women who could twist the landscape into another world if you lost your footing or strayed from the path.

She glanced back at the men, who were dawdling and talking loudly. The boy who didn't talk much was weaving drunkenly from side to side. Jenny scowled, deciding that they were all selfish and stupid, far too busy pouring their wages down their throats to care about the safety of the young woman waiting for them.

'Is there nowhere closer?' Graham the Scotsman asked again.

'*No.*'

'No carts to carry us? We're resourceful men, we could borrow a cart from somebody, then get a donkey–'

'Nope. No donkeys 'round here. Certainly none who could haul fifteen drunk men on a single cart. I promise, it's really not far. You could probably find it yourself. It's just a mile along the coast to the farm with the red barn door.'

'Are you *sure* there's no donkeys? I heard this whole island was covered in donkeys. I'm sure we could borrow some donkeys. Why doesn't your father have donkeys?'

'I don't know, because they'd eat the tomatoes?'

'We should get paid extra, having to walk miles until–'

'It's just *one* mile. A *single* mile, to a farm with a red barn door, and we'd get there a lot faster if you gentlemen just walked a bit quicker. Oh hell, did one of the gravediggers just fall in the ditch? Could somebody help him please?'

They had walked perhaps five minutes along the path before one of the cousins from Alderney shouted, 'Look over there!'

Jenny's shoulders drooped as the rest of the men first staggered to a halt, then wandered off the lane in the wrong direction to see where he was pointing.

'What now?' Jenny sighed.

'It's a horse!' One of the vraic gatherers stumbled to the side so that she could see past him.

Sure enough, there on the beach was a horse, trotting across the sand towards them and then up the low hill over the heather.

It was a magnificent creature. Flawless black, without markings. Its coat shone with the copper light of reflected sunset, burnishing its long mane so that it looked aflame. It was as tall as a carthorse, but much more graceful, its long legs slender and built for speed.

'That's a fine-looking mare,' said the other cousin from Alderney.

'Where did you escape from, pretty lady?' Jenny asked.

The mare had no halter, but her condition suggested she was healthy and extremely well-cared for.

The horse arched her neck as she walked into the group of men and shook her head, black mane cascading around her shoulders.

'Well, aren't you the most beautiful girl?' Jenny smiled as the horse whickered softly.

'I'm gonna ride it,' Graham the Scotsman announced. 'I'm a resourceful man, and if a horse just turns up, I'm gonna ride it!'

'No you aren't. We bloody spotted it.' The cousins from Alderney both moved closer to the mare, and one took a handful of her mane.

'It's not your horse to ride, any of you,' Jenny said, putting her hand to her forehead and rubbing her eyes with exasperation as the tomato pickers began to gather around the mare.

'If it doesn't even have a bridle,' one of the vraic gatherers said, 'it might not belong to anybody anyway. Might be wild.'

'There aren't any wild horses in Guernsey, and since it doesn't have a bridle how are you expecting to guide it, exactly?' Jenny doubted anybody heard her over the disagreement that was breaking out over who would ride the horse.

She stepped forward, reaching past the boy who didn't say much to pat the horse's head. Against her fingers the horse's elegant nose was as soft as black velvet.

'If you kick any of them,' she whispered to the mare, 'I will completely understand.'

The boy stepped away and Jenny looked into the mare's eyes. Her fingers stilled on the horse's forehead as she met its gaze and her smile faded from her lips.

It whickered again softly, lifting its head to mouth her fingers gently, but Jenny pulled away and stepped back. For what kind of a horse had eyes the deep blue green of a stormy sea? Its gaze glittered with a cool intellect. The black pupils of its eyes were … *wrong* somehow. Not quite like a cat, but not like a horse either. Not at all like a horse, Jenny thought. The horse blinked slowly and there was something in the curve of its mouth. Almost a smile or, as it flicked its gaze to the men who were surrounding it, perhaps a sneer. The white teeth that flashed were not like the teeth of a horse.

The sun sank beneath the horizon and the sky turned to a purple bruise, with clouds of deep, dark pink, like blood in water.

'I think we should go,' Jenny said sharply, but the men were disagreeing with the obtuse extreme volume that only drunk men and babies are capable of. 'I'm tired!' Jenny yelled. 'Leave the horse, and let's go!'

One of the men from Alderney still held a handful of the horse's mane and, with a leg up from his cousin, he hauled himself onto its back. There was a cheer and then he pulled his cousin up behind him. The horse remained still, apparently unconcerned with the weight of two grown men on her back. Graham the Scotsman was still protesting that it had been his idea to ride.

'It's a big bloody horse,' he was complaining, 'it can carry three for sure!'

It was a big horse, Jenny realised with a shiver. It was bigger than a carthorse. Bigger even than she'd thought. Possibly bigger than it had been when it first trotted up to them. The black mare turned a slow circle with the two men on its back, its shoulders broader than a bull's.

'You can't have three men on a horse!' Jenny said, but the Scotsman was already dragging himself up behind the cousins from Alderney. His flailing leg caught the horse's flank hard, but the creature did not flinch or stir.

'Get down!' Jenny shouted, but the Scotsman just crowed with laughter.

'Look at the size of this thing! Bloody great brute.' He managed to swing his leg over and extended a hand. 'It'll easily take four – here lad, grab my arm.'

He grabbed the boy who didn't say much and pulled him up as hard as he could. The boy, who was much the worse for drink, was pulled head and shoulders over the horse's back. He continued to slide over it entirely and landed on his face in the long grass on the other side.

The horse turned its head, pricked up its ears and looked at the fallen boy thoughtfully. A ripple shivered along its ribs and Jenny wondered if it was amused. The men certainly were. The boy's fall occasioned much hilarity, slapping of knees and shouts of laughter, even before it was established that he was unhurt. He was pushed up again by the other men, and this time he managed to retain his seat.

Jenny, still slowly edging backwards, shook her head when one of the gravediggers held up his hand and was dragged up next.

The horse still did not appear to feel any discomfort from its burden of five drunk riders. She watched it step closer to the other men – practically *inviting* them, Jenny realised.

'That's enough!' she said harshly. 'This is cruel. Get down, now! Let's go!'

She didn't really expect them to pay attention to her, and they didn't. Drunk men rarely pay attention to advice that doesn't suit them, and farmhands never listened to the farmer's daughter.

She jumped nervously as she backed into something behind her, turned to see a high white stone, and flinched away from it. Perhaps it was just a boundary stone, but perhaps it was a faery stone, one of those said to twist the land into another place than this world. These were things the islanders were supposed to remember. Don't touch the stones. Don't look at giant black dogs. Don't leave the paths. Don't go looking for goblin gold. Stay away from strange lights at night, especially blue ones, and … wasn't there something about horses?

Jenny smoothed down her shirt and trousers, and tried to compose herself and breathe steadily. Faery stones and giant horses that had eyes as green as the depths of the sea were not good things. She was half-tempted to abandon the drunk men entirely and run home. She looked back to see another man being hauled onto the horse's back, and this time there was no doubt that the horse had grown even while she had been distracted. Its shoulders were broader, and its legs were longer and thicker, with corded muscle like a racing stallion. Another man was struggling up, raising shouts of protest and laughter as he grabbed handfuls of the mounted men's clothing and kicked somebody while swinging his leg over their heads.

The laughter of the men infuriated Jenny. Had this been a normal horse, even a giant carthorse, this treatment would be unspeakably cruel. Its back would have bent under their selfish weight. It would be distressed, it would buck and rear and neigh and tremble, and would they even care?

This horse stood patiently. As tall and fine as any horse that ever walked the earth. Stronger, and wilder, with eyes glittering in the dying light.

'Get down!' she shouted. 'Get off her! What is wrong with you people? Can't you see there's something wrong with this horse? Why won't you listen to me?'

The second gravedigger leapt up. He half pulled down the boy who didn't say much, but then both of them were awkwardly hauled upright, amidst laughter. Another man was pulled up, legs flailing, for the horse's back was higher now than it had been before. Its growth had been slow enough that its drunken riders had somehow not noticed.

One of the Frenchmen exploded in curses as he was elbowed in the face. This was also found to be a source of great amusement.

The horse, malachite eyes blazing in its huge skull, turned patiently and flicked its mane. The mare was so tall now that the men on the ground had to reach up to their fullest height just so that the other tomato pickers could lean down and clasp their hands. Hauling up the last men was a harder business still, and they did not consider the horse, either its size or how absurd it was to expect one animal to carry fifteen men. One of the brothers from Sark ended up sitting the wrong way around on a Frenchman's lap, and their shouting and laughter became as loud as it had been in the bar.

The horse still did not show any discomfort. It bent one powerful front leg and lifted an unshod hoof as large as a cartwheel. This served as a useful step for the last two unsteady drunkards to clamber more easily onto its massive back. It was probably bigger than any horse that had ever lived now, Jenny thought. It was surely bigger than an elephant. More powerful and more terrifying. If it had been a real horse, it would have been worth a king's ransom for its size and astonishing beauty.

The last of the light was fading and the world was turning to silver and grey. The black horse, with its fifteen drunk riders, walked to Jenny's side and looked down at her with its fathomless blue-green gaze. It lifted its hoof and dipped its shoulder invitingly. When it blinked its long black lashes, it looked amused.

'No thank you,' Jenny whispered as the riders laughed and reached for her. She danced back a few steps to get away from them.

'Told you we were resourceful,' Graham the Scotsman hiccupped before continuing. 'If you're too precious to share the horse, walk ahead and lead us to the place.'

Some of the men were kicking at the horse, digging their heels and yelling for it to *walk on*.

'No thank you,' Jenny said again to the horse.

It dipped its head once. A very human nod of understanding. Then it turned, rearing slightly. There was shouting, but none of the men fell from its back. The horse broke into a canter, heading back the way it had come. Down through the heather and the rough grass towards the beach it ran. The cousin sitting at the front made some vague effort to guide it, yelling and pulling on its mane. The horse went as it pleased, heading towards the dying light as it began to race into a gallop. Its mane was a pennant of shadow that seemed to wrap around its riders as it headed for the sea.

'They'll all be drowned,' Jenny whispered.

Her hands flew to her mouth as she watched, remembering childhood tales of the kelpies. They were monsters who looked so much like horses, until some fool tried to ride them. Then the kelpies ran and dived and swam with the helpless, confused riders clinging and confined, trapped by magic as they were pulled beneath the waves and murdered by their mounts. They weren't horses at all, but waterhorses, fée creatures who were wild and wily water-predators with sharp teeth. They were either black as the ocean depths, or sea-foam white. Creatures who shape-shifted and grew fins when they entered the water.

There was nothing Jenny could do but watch the kelpie hurtle towards the silver line of the lowering tide. Its hooves churned piles of black seaweed and wet grey sand, then sprays of water as it entered the shallows.

Then it stopped.

It stopped as suddenly as a horse refusing a jump.

Its head dipped as it skidded to a halt, its front legs splayed in front of it. Fifteen drunk men, carried forward by the momentum of a huge horse at a hard gallop, were launched at full speed into the air.

They flew high, seeming to spin and flail for long moments, their ungainly limbs all tangled, before they landed hard in grey mud and knee-deep water.

Jenny winced as she saw some of them land face first, or under the weight of others. There was a moment of silent shock, and then they were drenched and wailing, cursing and roaring with pain and discomfort. There was the wretched screaming of a broken arm, the weeping misery of a bruised back, and yelling about a sprained or broken ankle. There was also the loud vomiting of someone for whom the spinning impact had proven too great to hold their drink. For the most part, at this distance, Jenny could not make out who was who, save for variously accented shouting.

She smiled when she realised it was Graham the Scotsman who had broken his arm.

The boy who didn't say much was suddenly wailing a stream of curses and vile profanity and attempting to throw seaweed at the kelpie. The kelpie watched his futile efforts, with pricked ears and a tilted head, before frisking around like a huge puppy and then beginning to gallop along the edge of the water, mane and tail whipping, sending spray flying. It reduced in size as it ran, gradually becoming once again the size of a normal horse.

It turned inland and kicked its heels joyously, tossing its head and leaping like a show pony, enjoying its own speed and beauty and delighting in the stupidity of humans, before arcing back around and heading once more for the men gradually picking themselves out of the mud. It slowed as it approached them and Jenny was relieved that now, at least, they had the sense to try to stay away from it, stumbling back and falling out of its path. All except one vomiting Frenchman on his knees.

It trotted past them, tossing its head proudly, as it entered the sea. It went deeper, and deeper, surging through the water, until it was swimming. At last, it dipped its head under the surface of the silver sea and dived. The arch of its back showed a ridge of fin, and the kick of its heels showed a fan of webbing above the hooves.

Jenny watched the ripples on the water recede, barely noticing the drunken shouting of the men in the shallows, who were pulling each other up and arguing about whose stupid idea it had been to ride the horse.

Some were calling out to her. Apparently they had not bothered to remember her name. They were calling, 'Farmer's girl!' in increasingly insistent and angry voices.

Jenny sniffed, tilted her head thoughtfully and then shouted over to them.

'You're resourceful! I'm sure you'll find your way!'

Then she turned and walked home.

LA VIOGE

Beyond this place of wrath and tears
Looms but the Horror of the shade,
And yet the menace of the years
Finds and shall find me unafraid.

William Ernest Henley

Camila had to knock on the door three times before it was yanked open by the sullen farmer. Though English was her second language, she spoke it perfectly, and she asked him very politely if he would mind changing his scarecrow.

The scarecrow was scaring her young son terribly when he walked home from school, she explained. A young girl had gone missing in the neighbourhood, and everyone was on edge after searching for her with no success. No sign of her had been found, except for her broken silver necklace. The girl, Alisa, had been her son Gabriel's schoolfriend. He was upset enough without some ragged scarecrow giving him nightmares.

The farmer knit his heavy brow and said something Camila could not understand in the Jersey-French language. She did not speak Jèrriais, but she knew a few words of French, and struggled to make herself understood. She knew the new lighthouse in the West of the island was named for crows, so she tried saying, '*L'homme de la corbière?*'

The farmer shrugged and shook his head, lower lip protruding obstinately and tried to wave her away. Camila suspected that the farmer understood English very well, so she jammed her hand foot in the door as he tried to close it. She offered to redress the scarecrow herself, to change how it looked, so that her son would find it less frightening.

The farmer wrenched the door fully open, leaned close and said in heavily accented English, 'I do not *have* a scarecrow. No birds here.'

Then he slammed the door.

Indeed, as Camila walked slowly up the narrow, high-sided lane beside the field that was called *La Ruette à la Vioge*, she could not see a scarecrow. She climbed up the high bank a couple of times to look across the field, but it seemed to be empty save for the lush green of ripening wheat. She wondered why her son Gabriel had been so troubled by the idea of a scarecrow. He had been pale when he talked about it. Perhaps he had only seen it in a nightmare.

The lane was more of a high-sided footpath, the field on one side and a high bank with arching trees on the other. It looked like a steep tunnel. Golden and green, with sunlight-dappled ground and lush foliage. The lane was silent except for the whispering breeze. As the farmer had said, there were no crows, and no sparrows twittered in the trees. She decided it must be the unusual heat driving the birds to more shadowed places.

'The scarecrow is gone,' she told Gabriel when he came home from school.

After running upstairs and looking from a high window, which looked out across the fields, her son agreed that it was gone. He smiled and looked relieved.

But as Gabriel prepared for bed that night, just as darkness fell completely, he looked out and saw a figure in the distance. It was closer than the night before, dressed and hooded in ragged clothes.

He called for his mother, but by the time she arrived to calm him, nightfall was almost complete. She could not see where he pointed, so could only hug him and assure him that a scarecrow could do him no harm.

For the past few months Gabriel's great aunt had been living with them. A stroke had diminished her ability to move or speak, and left her in a state of some confusion. Camila had insisted that she moved in with them until she was able to take care of herself again.

Gabriel had not known his aunt very well before she moved in, and found it hard to understand her. He was, perhaps, a little afraid of her. It was uncomfortable to see another person struggle to form words, or to stand, or to eat her food without help.

He was as kind to her as he knew how to be. He would stand awkwardly and tell her about each day at school. He sometimes read to her from her own books because she could no longer turn the pages, and his mother did not always have time. The stories were boring and romantic, and none of the characters ever seemed to do anything but talk and travel in a coach. There were endless descriptions of countryside and mountains and ballrooms, but he could see by her crooked smile that she was pleased. He sat with her often, when he would rather be outside or reading his own books.

'Family takes care of family,' his father had said, patting Gabriel on the head, but his father was a sailor and was often away from home for weeks at a time.

Since the disappearance of the little girl weeks before, the old woman had been agitated, often trying to rise and stand unsteadily near the window. Camila had to guide her back to her seat, where she would sit, shaking from the exertion and forcing out words. Her speech was slurred but Gabriel kept hearing her repeat the same words.

'*The hot summers. Only in the hot summers.*'

Gabriel had started walking the long way home so that he did not have to go up Crack Ankle Lane. That was what the other children called *La Ruette à la Vioge* because it was so steep. Gabriel had sometimes walked home with Alisa, the little girl who had gone missing. He had been late leaving the school the afternoon she had disappeared – he was kicking around a ball with some of the other boys as she left, and she had never been seen again.

Then, a few mornings later, when he had been about to set out for school, he had looked out over the fields. He had seen what he thought was a scarecrow, but when he looked again its head was turned towards him. A fraction of a difference, the slightest suggestion of change, but he had felt a sudden dread that he could not explain. It had caused him to turn and run and find another path over different fields to get to school. He had been late, but his teacher had seen the bloodless fear on his face and quickly forgiven his tardiness.

Now for three nights he had seen the scarecrow from his bedroom window as the world turned dark, and it was closer each time. Despite the intense heat of the June nights, Gabriel shut his window and pulled the covers over his head. He suffered from the heat and slept very little.

On the fourth evening, it was not in the field before he went in for dinner.

'Any sign of your scarecrow?' his mother asked him gently as he sat down.

Gabriel knew she was trying to make him laugh his fear away and forced a weak smile.

His Great Aunt Ana became distressed at his mother's words. She started trying to say something that neither of them could understand until, frustrated, she banged her hands down on the table. A tear slid down her cheek.

'I'm so sorry but I cannot understand you, Aunty,' his mother said sadly.

His Aunt Ana kept croaking a word, '*Vioge*.' It was a sound neither of them had ever heard before.

After dinner, when Gabriel was trying to read to Aunt Ana, she grabbed his sleeve with a firm and shaking grip. With wild eyes she said, slowly, 'Silver... and salt... and old... cold iron.'

Gabriel nodded, though he did not understand what she wanted, or what she might be trying to tell him. Sometimes she did not make sense, but it seemed important to her, so he nodded as she repeated it again with her obstinate, awkward lips. '*Silver. Salt. Old, cold iron.*'

'Yes, Aunty Ana. Silver and salt and old cold iron. I'll remember the words. Shall I read to you some more?'

He continued reading, but he did not think she was listening anymore. She was just staring at him. When his mother went upstairs, Aunt Ana struggled up and moved unsteadily to the cupboards. Gabriel stood near her in case she fell and called for his mother. By the time Camila came back down, his great aunt had located the salt cellar and was shaking it into his hands and hers. As his mother arrived, he thanked his great aunt for the palmful of salt and put it uncertainly in his pocket when she gestured for him to do so.

That night he woke in a terror. His blanket was pulled back and a figure was standing above him. He shouted in panic and his mother ran in swiftly with a lantern. His great aunt was leaning over him, her gnarled fingers shaking like she was bestowing a curse.

'What is she doing?' Gabriel asked.

'It's salt Gabriel, she's just shaking salt onto you,' his mother said.

Biting her lip, Camila led his aunt gently back to her room.

The salt stung oddly. Prickling Gabriel's skin in an annoying way. He sat up and tried to brush it off, but grains had crept down his back. A delicate breeze touched his skin and he frowned and squinted. The window was open.

Fear spiked in his stomach and he stood. Music reached his ears; a single note that hung on the air like a soft flute. Gabriel reeled with exhaustion and sat down on the bed, trying to hold on to the determination to close the window. The music was lovely. He just wanted to lay down and listen to it. A pleasant scent, like gorse-flowers, floated in on the breeze.

The salt, hot as tiny embers, began to burn his skin. The music grew louder and tiredness tugged at him, but the salt like little bee stings kept him from falling back to sleep. Gabriel stood and stumbled over to the window.

In the weak moonlight he could see a black shape against the deep grey of moonlit clouds. The scarecrow was closer than it had ever been, and its strange music was rising, filling him with unbearable fatigue. The salt burned like dropped matches and Gabriel slammed the window shut, latched it, and fell to his knees like a drunk.

His mother shook him awake the next morning. Concern lined her face to find him asleep on the floor by the window, but he assured her he was well. He was surprised to find that the grains of salt, which had burned so hot the night before, had left no marks at all against his skin.

He stumbled late into school. He was given a note to take home to his parents when he fell asleep at his desk. He took the long way home and yawned through dinner as though he hadn't slept at all the night before.

His mother forgave him for the note and talked as they ate. A young farm worker had gone missing, people said, but who knew if a young man might not just walk away from a hard job one night and take a boat home? No one could be sure if the boy was missing like the little girl, or whether he had simply found better work elsewhere.

Gabriel looked blankly at the silver ring his aunt pressed into his hands when his mother stepped away to boil water for tea. He began to refuse it and hand it back. He relented when he saw the trembling of her hands and the urgency in her watery eyes. Then he thanked her. It was about the scarecrow, he realised. His aunt knew something was hunting him.

'Vioge,' she said again.

'Is that what it's called?' Gabriel asked. 'The monster in the field? And what you said about salt, silver and iron… do they protect us?'

She managed a relieved nod when she saw that he understood. She held up three crooked fingers and it took him a while to guess that she meant the monster always took three people. Alisa was the first and the young farm worker was probably the second. There was a silent understanding between Gabriel and his aunt that his mother would not believe a monster lurked in the fields in plain sight. A monster that only appeared in the hottest summers and took three people away.

Gabriel kept the ring in his pocket until night began to fall, then slipped it onto the middle finger of his left hand. He also went to the kitchen and put a pinch of salt on his head. He checked that the front and back door were locked, then sat and waited on his bed as the light faded. Waiting with his teeth clenched for his mother to go to sleep so that he could shut the window without argument. He felt the song even before he heard it. The sudden heaviness of his limbs, the involuntary drop of his chin to his chest.

The ring was like bitter ice on his finger. It felt like part of his hand was submerged in a freezing lake. His head prickled like bees were stinging him, and still the exhaustion made his eyelids droop. He made himself stand up. He closed the window quietly as he yawned and staggered, then he took two unsteady steps back to bed, and collapsed.

Something leaned over him…

It was his aunt checking on him, patting his head with awkward, gentle hands as he murmured an exhausted good night to her.

Something leaned over him…

His mother, sighing and softly remonstrating that it was too hot for his window to be closed. He protested sleepily, but the moment slipped away into dark dreams of dipping his hands in an ice bucket and being stung on his scalp by angry bees.

Something leaned over him…

A face of haggard, ancient skin tattered and torn as rotted cloth. A gaping mouth that stretched impossibly wide. Its soporific song ceased, and it began to inhale. Gabriel felt something start to tear inside his chest and rise up his throat, like his breath was being sucked from within his lungs.

The ring burned like cold, white lightning. The salt seared his scalp like hot pokers.

Gabriel screamed and rolled from the bed onto the floor. He reached into his pyjama pocket and threw salt at the vioge.

This time the salt did burn. Everywhere it touched *la vioge* it sparked and popped like gunpowder. The monster whipped back. It was a single motion almost too fast to see. With one burst of terrifying speed, it made up for all the long hours of standing so utterly and completely still. If it could perform such explosions of movement, Gabriel thought, how could he ever run from it?

Gabriel screamed again, screamed for his father, but his father was far, far away at sea.

It was his mother who came running.

The vioge flashed away again, and was gone through the window, out into the night. It was long gone by the time his mother arrived a moment later to gather him into a hug and start talking about nightmares.

Gabriel began to shout at her, wild and furious, to tell her that it was not a nightmare. To shout that she had let something inside their home by opening the window. He shook free of her embrace and slammed the window shut with such force that she jumped. He could see he was frightening her, but in his panic he could not stop yelling. He told her it was her fault, and that she did not listen.

He could see that she thought him in the grip of some night terror, and that the louder he shouted, the more convinced she became that he was being irrational.

'Why does it smell like burning in here?' she asked.

She was so upset and confused that he sat down on the floor with his face in his hands, trying not to weep. Appalled and exhausted, he was on the verge of despair. Then his great aunt was there, kneeling beside him, and he threw himself into her arms. His breathing was rough and ragged with misery, but he refused to cry.

He did not sleep again that night. He sat and turned the ring on his finger until dawn touched the fields with russet gold. He knew that sunlight did not really make him safer – his friend Alisa had been taken in the daytime, but at least he could see whether the vioge was out there. As darkness retreated the worst of the suffocating terror went with it, and there was no sign of the vioge in the fields.

'Where can I get iron?' He asked his mother when she came down to breakfast a few hours later. His eyes were dark as pits and his fingers trembled. She did not ask him why he wanted it. She just listed everything she could think of that was made of iron. An old horseshoe, almost rusted through, was found nailed to the garden shed.

'Keep it with the ends up. Like a smile,' she said as he placed it on the windowsill. 'So the luck doesn't run out of it.'

She pointed out that the poker and tongs beside the fireplace were iron and helped him find a ribbon to hang an old, unused gate key around his neck. The key was reassuringly heavy.

'We'll keep the window closed tonight,' Camila said gently.

He nodded and thanked her, wondering whether it would make any difference.

'We must try not to wake Aunty Ana up in the night, Gabriel,' she said gently. 'She needs her sleep if she's going to get better.'

'I know. I'm sorry.' Gabriel hugged her fiercely. 'And I'm sorry I shouted at you.'

'I think you better stay home from school today, Gabriel.'

He thanked her, but he was distressed to learn that his mother planned to go into town. He only became calmer when she informed him that she would be getting a lift there and back in the horse-drawn cart belonging to the old couple who lived up the road.

'It's not so hot today. I think the weather might be turning,' she said as she left. 'We'll sleep better tonight, Gabriel.'

The vioge did not wait until nightfall.

Gabriel was making tea for his great aunt when a wave of sound washed over him. He almost collapsed, knocking one of the cups to the floor where it smashed, loud and startling. He grabbed the table with one hand, to steady himself, and pressed the other hand to the gate key that rested against his chest. Where the iron touched his skin a cool, sharp sensation radiated outwards like thorns clawing over him. As it spread, he heard the truth of the vioge's enchanting music. Stripped of magic and glamour it was a hoarse, rasping roar. The ravenous death rattle was accompanied by a smell that no longer seemed as sweet as gorse-flowers, but instead stank like a charnel house.

His aunt pointed a wavering finger out the window and he saw the vioge waiting in the field, once again as still as a scarecrow. Its raw mouth was wide open. Only the barest suggestion of life glittered in its deep, black eye sockets.

Gabriel ran to draw the curtains, throwing the room into shadow, and helped his aunt up to her room where they shut the door. He slid down to the floor while she sat trembling on the bed.

'It won't stop, will it?' Gabriel asked. 'If it always takes three people. If it wants me...?'

She shook her head, held up her hands and he could see she did not know.

The music of the vioge lifted in the air and his aunt's eyes closed. She dropped, limp, against her pillows. For a moment Gabriel was ter-rified that she was dying, but then he saw the steady rise and fall of her chest and knew that it was only the cursed sleep of the vioge's song.

The iron key prickled like a briar patch, and he was glad of it, because this time he managed to stay awake through the exhaustion. How long could somebody stay awake before they went mad, he won-dered? Would being awake even make a difference if the monster lost patience? Was there any amount of salt, silver or iron that could defeat it? Could he convince people to help him fight? How could anyone fight something that moved with the speed of a swooping falcon? How could somebody even get close enough?

The questions troubled him even when the soporific song stopped.

His aunt looked weary when she woke from her unnatural slumber. She looked like a woman who had been drugged. She was confused and struggling harder to find her balance. Far worse than she had been in months. It made him bitterly sad and angry to see her so weak again.

She looked even more tired and worried than he felt.

'I'll stay safe, Aunty Ana,' he said, holding her hands and staring into her amber eyes earnestly. 'I'll put salt across the window ledges and the doorways. I'll wait for it with the poker. I won't let it take me without a fight, I promise.'

His mother frowned with concern when he heard the cart and raced out to help with the groceries. He rushed her back inside the house, carrying all the bags for her. She did not mistake his fear for solicitude.

He agreed that he would go with her to see the doctor, as long as she promised to stay inside for the next few days. She did not argue when Gabriel checked all the windows and doors were locked tight behind them. They all sat down to a near-silent evening meal, and for the first time in a long time Ana shook so badly that Camila had to help her with her food.

In the field, in the distance, the scarecrow stood motionless.

Natural exhaustion made Gabriel's eyelids heavy. He splashed water on his face, sprinkled salt down his back, and tapped his ringed finger against the iron key at his neck. He dozed uneasily on the couch as his mother read to his aunt, resting his eyes, and trying to think of ways to fight back, jerking fully awake every few minutes.

Silver and salt and old, cold iron.

Only the hottest summers.

Three people. Always three people.

A candle was lit. His mother covered him with a light blanket and reassured him that the windows and doors were locked, and that his aunt was going to sit up with him for a little while.

His aunt sprinkled him with salt when his mother went up to bed and the salt did not sting his skin.

The candlelight moved and the key did not prickle against his chest.

A door closed softly but the ring did not feel cold on his finger.

He slept the night through until he was woken in the morning by his mother calling for his aunt. He woke in a panic and tore the blanket away. He knew from his mother's worried face that Ana was not in the house.

'*No!*' Gabriel ran for the door, sprinting out into the cool morning air and into the field.

The wheat was damp with dew, cold against his hands as he followed the faint line where it had been disturbed, the uneven shadow of a path. He could imagine his aunt's unsteady steps as he had slept and she had walked, awkward and afraid but determined, into the night.

He saw something black upon the ground and cried out, but it was just clothing. His mother was there behind him, pulling him back, lifting him with shocking strength to protect him from any sight that she could not bear her son to see.

'It's just her shawl!' he shouted. 'Mum, it's just her shawl!'

Gabriel dropped down next to it as his mother walked deeper into the field calling Ana's name.

He knew she would not find Ana.

On the shawl, in a little pile, were Ana's silver rings. Her necklace was snapped. She would not have been able to work the delicate clasp with such traitorously awkward fingers, and she had wanted to take it off. She had wanted to make herself easier to hunt. She had given herself to the monster in his place.

Always three. Gabriel's vision blurred with tears.

'She must have been confused,' his mother said, 'She's probably just wandered away. We'll find her, Gabriel.'

'We won't,' he said quietly. 'We won't find her. She wasn't confused. She was *brave*. She was brave and she did this to save me. But *why* would she do that? I could have *fought*, mum. I could have fought the vioge!'

Gabriel stood with her shawl clasped to his chest, trying to swallow sobs. Hot tears ran down his cheeks as he looked around, turning as the dawn haze cleared and sunlight grazed golden fingers slowly across the wheat. There was nothing for miles around but green fields and trees, as the birds began to sing.

Hearth Faeries

Last night I saw upon the stair
A little man who wasn't there
He wasn't there again today
Oh, how I wish he'd go away…

Hughes Mearns

The first time Harriet was sure they had a house elf was when she knocked a glass from the table by accident. She had leant across to reach for the salt, but as she sat back her elbow caught her wine glass and sent it spinning from the table to the floor. She exclaimed with dismay and winced with the certain expectation of glass shattering.

There was only silence. When she looked down the glass was upright and still half full. It stood perfectly undamaged, in a spattered puddle of spilled wine. Something unseen, with extraordinarily swift reactions, had plucked it from the air halfway through its fall and set it down.

Harriet stared at it for a while, sitting with her head to one side as her food went cold.

'What's the matter with you?' Her brother James slapped his hand on the table to get her attention.

'Nothing,' Harriet said quickly, leaning down to retrieve her glass. 'Absolutely nothing at all.'

There had been other things.

Harriet had left a dress, with a tear in the skirt, on a chair by the fire one night. She had begun to sew it, but dim candlelight and tired eyes had made her give up halfway through. Sucking her finger after she'd stabbed herself with a needle, she had sworn in a most unladylike fashion and gone up to bed.

In the morning the dress had been mended with such tiny, flawless stitches it was almost hard to see where it had been damaged at all. She had asked her brother whether he had sewn the dress. He had told her, with a look of extreme disdain, that sewing was a woman's work. Most things were a woman's work in James's opinion. However, since he had solely inherited their parents' house, Harriet lived there on his sufferance. So she bit her lip and did far more than her fair share, without asking for anything. She had nowhere else to go. She knew she was a plain girl, with plain dresses. She had no money of her own and no prospects of finding a husband, since she rarely left the house. There was a farm worker, Stephen, who had a smile that made her blush, but why would he be interested in her? She kept her head down whenever he called at the house to speak to James.

It wouldn't matter even if Stephen did like her. James's pride was too great to let his sister marry a simple farm worker. Besides, without a sister to treat as a drudge, James would have had to hire a housekeeper, which would cost him far more money.

At first Harriet thought the missing cheese, apples, and slices of cake were just James helping himself to food at odd hours. Darned socks and finished knitting, however, were not oddities that could be attributed to her brother so easily.

'If you're not going to finish that, I'll have it.' James pointed at her pie with his fork and Harriet set the wine glass back on the table.

'No, no, I'm just eating slowly,' Harriet insisted, but when she went to bed, she left the last piece of her pie on the hearth to keep it warm. In the morning the pie was gone and the plate was washed, and she laughed aloud.

'*Thank you*,' she said, spinning around, looking for any glimpse of their elusive guest. 'Thank you for everything you do!'

She began sewing a patchwork quilt. She found a strange delight in leaving square pieces cut and ready when she went up to bed, then finding them flawlessly stitched into place the next day.

Alone and lonely most days, Harriet began speaking aloud about matters that were on her mind. Sometimes she would read aloud in the evening, softly so her brother didn't hear. It was at these times that she most sensed someone was there. Sometimes the hair would stand up on her neck, for she knew that faery folk, even the helpful ones, are often very powerful.

One night she apologised, with a sigh, that the bread and butter and cheese that she was leaving out must seem a little dull for a faery. She explained that her brother, who saw no issue with buying expensive wines and throwing money away over games of cards, expected her to make the housekeeping money stretch rather further than was possible. Then he would complain when meals weren't exactly to his taste.

The next day, when she put her hand into her apron pocket she found a small gold coin. After that she made sure to bake more cakes, as the House Brownie seemed to have a sweet tooth. She judged that it was quite small, since the portions eaten were always quite little.

One night, unable to sleep, she slipped down to the kitchen in the darkness for a glass of milk, and something moved so swiftly she felt her nightdress ripple in the breeze and a dustpan and brush clattered and fell.

'I'm sorry!' she called out. 'Oh I'm *so sorry*. I didn't mean to startle you I was just…' She poured milk into a cup, then a little more into a saucer, which she set down on the hearth as she slumped into the rocking chair by the dying fire and sighed. 'I was just thinking about Stephen. The farm worker I was telling you about. That way he laughs, and his eyes crinkle up. Did you ever see him speaking with James? He's not the least bit afraid of my brother, you know. Even though Stephen's only my height and James is so deliberately intimidating to the workers. He's so rude to them, but Stephen doesn't care, he's just relentlessly cheerful. It's not that I want to be beautiful. I just wish I wasn't so…' Harriet gestured vaguely at herself. 'I wish I wasn't so *me*. Other girls get to cheat at these things, you know. They have pretty dresses and maids to dress their hair. They have rouge and stupid hats and all that paraphernalia. More important than *any* of those things, they get a chance to speak to people. People *other* than invisible friends who help with the housework, I mean.

'Thank you again for the coin. Apparently it was very old, but I suppose you know that? I bought some more things for the pantry and some fruit. You must help yourself of course. Oh, and I bought some more thread and a yard of the most *beautiful* fabric. It's a colour somewhere between lilac and cornflower. Oh! What was that?'

Harriet jumped with surprise at the sound of a quiet thump on the floor. She looked down to see that the book she had been reading each evening had been dropped next to her.

'I see, you want me to read. Yes of course, I'll light a candle and we'll do another chapter.'

James shook her awake the next morning with the words, 'Good grief, *what* have you done to your hair? You look ridiculous.'

Harriet blinked awake in confusion. She was still in the chair in front of the fire, and it took her a moment to realise that she had fallen asleep there with the book on her lap.

'My hair?'

'What have I told you about burning candles at all hours?' James pointed at the half-burned candle on the mantlepiece.

Harriet had no memory of blowing it out. She put a hand to her hair, and it felt strange. She stood and walked quickly to the hall mirror and laughed with surprise.

Her hair was braided and bound in the most intricate, elegant manner imaginable. It was plaited and then curled in shining locks that tumbled around her shoulders. A single spiral curl rested against her right cheekbone. It looked strangely golden, like sunlight was shining on it, no matter how she tilted her head.

'What are you gawping at yourself for?' James sneered.

Harriet looked at him and shrugged helplessly. She had hair dressed like a princess, but she was stood in a patched nightdress.

'I just thought I'd try something new?'

'Why?' James shook his head. 'Who's going to care? I'm going out. I won't be back for dinner.'

Harriet was still admiring the intricate coiffure of her hair when she heard a crash and a yell from the kitchen. She found her brother sprawled on the floor in the process of getting up.

'Did you fall?' Harriet asked him.

'No! Well, yes, obviously! What a stupid question. I tripped over a damn cat or something. You better not be feeding strays again, Harriet! I swear if I find it, I'll wring its neck.'

She waited until the door slammed to say softly, 'I'd trip him over too if I could. But you must be careful of him, you know. He's always been horrid, even when we were children. Please don't ever let him know you're here.

'But my hair!' she added. '*Thank* you. I'll put on my best dress today. Not that you'll be able to tell the difference. It's as old as all the others, and just as ill-fitting, but it will cheer me up to look my best.'

At lunchtime she was still smiling and humming. She was rolling pastry in the kitchen when there was a soft knock on the open door. She turned and froze, one floury hand halfway to her heart.

'Sorry to surprise you, Miss Harriet...' Stephen's smile lit his eyes. 'I was wondering whether I could trouble you for a glass of water?'

'Oh! You know my name?' Harriet felt herself blush as soon as the words left her mouth and quickly dusted her hands on a tea towel. 'Sorry! Yes, of course, Stephen, it's no trouble at all.'

Stephen leant against the doorframe. 'I always bring a bottle and put it on the wall,' he shrugged. 'Just now when I went to take a drink, it had fallen and spilled somehow.'

'Had it?' Harriet paused for a moment as she lifted the water jug. 'Had it really? That's... Well, how strange.'

'And usually there's a few old mugs by the well, but...' he shook his head. 'It seems they've gone missing. So I thought I might impose upon you.'

She walked over to him, hoping her hand was steady as she passed him the glass, 'It's really no imposition at all, Stephen. Any time you need anything, absolutely anything, please feel free... Would you care for a seat or, or some *lunch* perhaps? There's bread and cheese and there's some stew I could heat for you? I could make you a sandwich. Or if you'd prefer-'

She broke off when Stephen started laughing.

'I wouldn't dream of stepping muddy boots into your house. I would be grateful for a bite of whatever you're having though, provided you'd join me outside in the sun?'

It seemed that Stephen became more clumsy in the placement of his water bottle over the coming weeks. Harriet struggled to maintain a neutral expression at his cheerful confusion at continually finding his water spilled over.

One day he returned to her a handkerchief that he had found, caught on a bramble near where he was working, which was artfully embroidered with her name. Harriet had no recollection of ever seeing it before, but accepted it with solemn gratitude, as though it had always been a prized possession.

When he knit his brow one day and explained that he had buried his water bottle halfway up to its neck in the earth that morning, and still found it tipped over, Harriet was hard-pressed not to laugh.

'The poor man,' she whispered into the darkness of the kitchen as she set out a slice of apple pie and cream. 'You'll make him think he's gone mad. You must like him too then? You *must* like him, or you wouldn't be helping. Isn't he *wonderful?* You really are the very best friend anyone could ever have.'

Stephen returned regularly, sometimes even when his water wasn't spilled, just to bid her a good afternoon. He only came on days that James was not at home, she noticed. Often he brought his own lunch and invited her to join him outside. On one occasion he brought her a small bunch of lilacs that he said he had found growing on the walk to work. One drizzly day he even left his boots outside and joined her at the table, and then he made her laugh until she had to beg him to stop because her stomach hurt.

Harriet had left a plain blue dress hung up to air one evening, and the next morning found that it had been altered to fit her perfectly. The next night it was exquisitely embroidered with tiny winding lilac flowers on the hem and bodice. The effect was so lovely she had to wipe tears from her eyes.

Some nights, as she fell asleep, she felt her hair stir against her scalp and sleepily thanked her invisible friend. Her hair would have little flowers or ribbons woven into styles that were timelessly elegant by morning. She now woke with her skin glowing, and her lips delicately stained with the juice of some russet berry. She was radiant – but whether from love, friendship, faery magic, or the joy of a more excit-ing life, she could never be sure.

One night her brother accused her of squandering the housekeeping money on a new dress. She lost her temper trying to explain, over his drunk shouting, that he was pointing at an old dress with new alterations.

As he began to call her ungrateful, and a burden, Harriet, who had been growing furious, saw something that made her fists uncurl. She slowly relaxed and smiled as she watched a very expensive bottle of rum, on the dining table behind her brother, begin to slide in small increments towards the edge. By the time it smashed to the flagstones, and he spun in surprise to look at it, she found herself feeling delight-fully calm.

'If we're struggling for money, James, then perhaps you should be more careful with your things?' she suggested, before turning and heading up to bed.

The next day she sighed when it was too heavy with rain for any work to be done on the farm, because it meant that Stephen would not be there. She was changing the bedlinen, watching in amusement as a duster danced around the room from one surface to the next, when his familiar knock sounded at the kitchen door. She stood still in surprise for a long moment wondering why he would be there, until she felt a tug at her skirt.

'Oh! Of course, he'll be standing in the rain.' Harriet glanced at herself in the mirror, patted her hair, and hurried downstairs. She threw open the kitchen door with a smile, but felt it die on her lips as she saw his face.

'I shouldn't be here.' Stephen held up a hand in refusal as she tried to draw him inside. He was soaked and his short hair was plastered to his head. 'I don't want to get you in any trouble. Your brother came to my home this morning and fired me. One of the other workers mentioned to him that we had been having lunch together and… oh lord, don't cry, Miss Harriet! I can *easily* get other work that pays far better, I'll be fine. I only stayed so long because… please, Harriet, there's no need to be so upset!'

Harriet, convulsing with sobs, had sunk to the floor. She was quite inconsolable, clasping his wet hands, blinded with tears.

'Please,' she managed. '*Please* don't say that I can't see you anymore, Stephen, *please*.'

'Oh hell,' he muttered, and she felt his arms slide around her. 'Harriet, I could never give you the life you deserve, you know that. Even if your brother would agree to let us marry… which he wouldn't. Please get up, My Love, you know it's true.'

He half carried her to a chair at the kitchen table and cupped her face with his hands. 'I shouldn't have kept coming here. I didn't realise I would end up hurting you like this. I swear I didn't mean to. Please stop crying, Harriet, before I start too. Really, this is ripping my heart out. I kept coming to see you because… wait…' He detached himself eventually from her kiss and exhaled shakily. 'You're not making this easy, Harriet. You must know there's no way we can be together. You must always have known that?'

Harriet shook her head. 'No, Stephen, please – there *must* be a way.'

He sat down on a chair and ran a hand over his wet hair. 'The only way for us is in disgrace, poverty and penury. A life you'd hate, and a choice you would definitely regret. I won't do that to you. I'm not that selfish.' He stood to go.

The kitchen door closed on its own. The key turned in the lock, dropped onto the floor with a clatter, and then slid under a cupboard as though kicked.

'What on earth…?' Stephen exclaimed.

'House brownie.' Harriet blew her nose violently on her embroidered handkerchief and hiccupped a sob, 'I suppose he doesn't want you to go either. Stephen, please, I promise I don't care about money. I'd rather live in a hole in the ground with you, than in a castle with any other man in the world.'

Stephen sat down slowly and smiled. 'That's the nicest thing anybody's ever said to me. *Really* though? It's a house elf? You're sure you're not just haunted?'

'Ghosts don't mend socks.'

She smiled as she watched Stephen laugh and look around the kitchen.

'You won't *ever* see him,' Harriet said. 'Not unless he wants you to. Sometimes there's a shadow or a flash of colour, but mostly I know he's here when things are mended or polished. He likes it when I read to him. Oh, and I always wake up looking like I'm ready to go to a ball.'

She pointed at her hair and Stephen raised an eyebrow, asking, 'Should I be jealous, Harriet?'

She leant against Stephen, and he put his arms around her.

'Your hair does always look magnificent. I liked it when you used to just tie it back with a blue ribbon too though.' He sat quietly, and then he said, 'Look, Harriet – my home is slightly more appealing than a hole in the ground, but not by much. Even if I was selfish enough to ask you to marry me, there's still the problem of your brother. He'd never consent. Perhaps in a year or two, if I work like a madman and you still haven't come to your senses…' He wiped one of her tears with his thumb. 'Perhaps we could elope then, but… what's wrong?'

Harriet had jumped up with a look of horror. 'James is home! Listen.'

The sound of hooves on cobbles made Stephen stand and sigh, and run his fingers through his wet hair again so that it stuck up in all directions.

'Is there any chance your invisible little friend is going to let me out of the house before your wretched brother punishes you for being alone with me?' he asked.

'We're not alone,' Harriet said and wiped her eyes with the heels of her palms. 'Anyway, I think it's time I spoke to James. Because if he thinks I'm going to cook and clean and change beds and act like his servant after he *dares* to try and take away the man that I love... Well, he's in for a surprise. Besides, if he throws me out into the street we'll *have* to get married won't we?'

Stephen's eyes crinkled with laughter. 'You'll be waiting a while before I can afford a ring, sweet Harriet, but I swear on my life I'll do everything I can to make you the happiest extremely poor woman alive.'

They were kissing as James walked into the kitchen, which was not calculated to put him in a good temper.

'You stupid, loose *slattern*,' he spat. 'As for you, Stephen Falle, I *told* you if I ever saw–'

Whatever he had been about to say to Stephen was forgotten when a plate suddenly hurled itself across the room and shattered inches from his head.

'Don't be rude, James,' Harriet said calmly as both men flinched and James staggered back. 'Stephen and I are getting married. He'll be your brother-in-law, so you should be happy for us.'

'*Happy* for you?' James turned. 'You will *never* marry this common-as-muck little–'

Another plate crashed against the wall.

'How are you doing that, you *Witch*?' James snarled at Harriet.

'Me?' Harriet held her hands up. 'I'm not doing anything. We have a house brownie. I don't think he likes you, but then...' She tilted her head thoughtfully. 'Really, what *is* there to like about you, James? You're lazy, you're rude, you're selfish, you're a penny-pincher and a gambler, you don't pay your employees enough and you are the most ungrateful–'

James started across the room with a meaningful stride. 'Liar! It's time I beat some sense into you.'

Stephen stepped swiftly in front of Harriet with his fists raised. It was an unnecessary gesture, since it was at that moment that the house brownie threw the kitchen table across the room.

It was an old, heavy oak table. The kind of table that four men would have strained to lift. The brownie tossed it with no more effort than it had thrown the plates. The table arced into the air, spun, and crashed to the floor inches from James's feet. James fell backwards and scrambled away as it rolled over once and settled on its side.

'Did you know it could do that?' whispered Stephen to Harriet.

'I didn't,' Harriet whispered back. 'Usually he just embroiders things and eats cake. Oh, and he knocked your bottle of water over *all the time*. I'm sorry. I swear I didn't ask him to do it, but I am very glad that he did.'

'Oh was *that* what was happening?' Stephen laughed. 'I thought that bottle was cursed or something.'

The shadows in the room were shifting, pouring into each other like drops of ink into water. A faint shape formed in the distortion of light, a figure no taller than a wineglass crouched on the table's edge, facing James. It shone with bright iridescence for an instant, then it was invisible again.

'He's never done that before,' Harriet said softly.

James was pale as death, teeth clenched as he pressed back against the wall.

'Fine then,' he said, his eyes still fixed on the spot the house brownie had disappeared from. 'Get out, both of you. Take that cursed little *thing* with you, or I'll find a way to kill it.'

'James, how could you? He's my friend!' Harriet's eyes filled with tears again.

James sneered at her. 'Know this, Harriet. You will walk out of this house with the clothes on your back and *nothing* more.'

'I suppose I shouldn't expect any better of you James,' Harriet wiped the tears rolling down her cheeks. She took Stephen's hand, but her husband-to-be didn't allow himself to be moved.

'Actually,' Stephen said, even-tempered as always, 'under the circumstances, James, I think I will expect better of you. After all, you miserable skinflint, Harriet is your *sister*. What will people say when they find out you kept her as a servant for half her life, and then forced her to marry into poverty without a dowry?'

'I don't *care*.'

'*More importantly*,' Stephen said. 'While your sister might get by on love…' Stephen gestured at the table. 'Imagine if my tatty little cottage doesn't appeal to our *marvellous* friend here. Maybe he'll decide he likes *this* house better and come back. I don't know if you've noticed, James, but he doesn't like you.'

'He tripped James once,' Harriet said helpfully.

'Really?' Stephen grinned. 'Well it's a shame he didn't trip him at the top of a flight of stairs. But then… I dare say it's not too late…'

'Get out,' whispered James, turning pale.

'No,' said Stephen calmly, '*You* get out. When your sister and I are properly married, she can come home with me. Until then, I won't have you terrorising my Harriet. Do be a good fellow for once, will you? Go and stay at an inn!'

'This is *my* house, and I will not be—'

A flagstone ripped out the floor, rose to eye-height and then smashed down with shattering force.

James scrambled past them to the kitchen door, tugged at it desperately until he realised it was locked, then turned and ran back out into the hall. They heard the front door slam.

Stephen smiled at Harriet. 'I'm sorry, my love. It's extremely bad manners of me to extort your brother and threaten him with a faery. I'm usually more polite, I promise. However, manners aren't worth much when I'm terrified my wife might regret marrying me.'

Harriet waved a dismissive hand. 'I'm not sure we need to worry overmuch about money to be honest, Stephen. I have become an excellent seamstress and a decent baker. Besides, the Brownie brings me these antique gold coins sometimes. I believe they might be faery gold. I'm not saying we should *expect* it from him, of course, but I don't think he'd ever let us *starve*.'

'The brownie brings you gold coins?' Stephen pulled Harriet into his arms and kissed her. 'You know, My Love, just a minute ago I thought I was the happiest man alive. But now, Harriet, *now* I am absolutely certain of it.'

LA BLIANCHE DANME

The fairies haunt this glade;–if one could catch
A glimpse of them and of their fairy queen–
Have our loud pastimes driven them all away?

Alfred, Lord Tennyson

'Please, Cassie, if I have to hear one more word about Flynn, I will pick up a twig and stab myself in both ears with it. You have been fixated on that boy for years. Can't we just enjoy these pretty woods? This is such a lovely little valley.'

Cassie made an exclamation of annoyance and started to walk ahead of her older sister down the path, turning only to say, 'I don't know why you are so determined to dislike him! What is so *wrong* with Flynn, I should like to know?'

'Nothing in particular,' Isobel sighed. 'But there is nothing particularly *right* with him either! He is handsome, yes, and he is a very charming flirt. Beyond that he has no substance. No particular wit or intelligence to recommend him. Besides which, he is often both loud and wrong at the same time, and his voice is really quite annoying. Oh, stop walking so fast! We can't leave our governess behind. Cassie, stop striding off like a dockworker. Cassie come *back*! The sun is going down. It could be dark before we reach the castle.'

Isobel threw up her hands as Cassie disappeared out of sight around a bend in the path. She turned to call back an apology to Madame Auffroy. Their ageing governess chaperoned them everywhere, and at an excruciatingly sedate pace. At first Isobel had politely tried to walk with her, but as Cassie had soon pointed out, this only encouraged Madame Auffroy to walk more slowly. 'It's like being trapped in a funeral procession!' her spirited sister had shouted one night.

Isobel trotted quickly after her sister, determined to keep her in sight. The shady path wound along the right side of the little valley. To Isobel's left a meadow full of grass and flowers was divided by a glittering stream. To her right a high bank of rock and trees stretched upwards in a high hill towards a blue sky. It had been a lovely crisp early spring afternoon, and Isobel regretted upsetting her sister.

'Cassie! Come back,' Isobel called, but as she ducked around a tree she almost ran directly into her sister, who was standing stock still.

'Isobel,' Cassie said urgently, grabbing her sister's hand. 'Is it just me, or is that lady glowing?'

Isobel had to step out around the tree and then past her sister to see what Cassie was talking about. She looked where her sister was staring, where the valley narrowed to a bottleneck, no more than a few strides wide. Shadows fell heavily over the path.

A woman stood there, dressed all in white, facing away from them. She stood like a queen, tall and proud and calm, with long golden hair that fell past her waist. Soft light made her luminous.

'She must just be stood in a patch of sunlight, Cassie. Women don't just… emanate light.'

'She hasn't moved since I saw her. And like you said, the sun's going down. Let's get closer.'

Isobel reached for her hand and tried to hold her back. Instead, Cassie determinedly pulled Isobel along with her, saying, 'Come on, Isobel! Quickly, before Madame Auffroy sees her and screams like a banshee, like she does whenever there's a spider. Do you think that woman is a *ghost*?'

'In the daylight? A day ghost? I never heard of anything like that. It must be a trick of the light. I don't think we should whisper. It seems rude. What if she can hear us?'

They approached, with careful steps. Cassie tiptoed as if she was sneaking up on a wild animal. Isobel tried to walk naturally while keeping her footsteps soft. As they drew closer it became clearer that the lady blocking their path was indeed glowing.

'What do we do?' Cassie whispered loudly.

Isobel winced, frowned at her, and then cleared her throat politely. 'Good afternoon!' she called with bright affability.

The woman in white turned slowly. Light seemed to spill from her, reflecting gold against the path and the steep rising slope of the valley. Her eyes were dark and very much alive. She raised a hand slowly, a greeting, and then left it raised, palm out and fingers spread, a wordless gesture that warned them to stop.

Cassie had already halted and was squeezing Isobel's hand so tightly that she tried to shake her fingers loose.

Cassie refused to let go. 'She's not a ghost, Isobel,' she hissed urgently, 'she's one of *le fée*, the fae people in the islands. Bry was talking about them. This is so exciting, Isobel! We must talk to her!'

'No Cassie, I think we should go back,' Isobel said firmly, she gave a polite nod to the fée lady, who was turning away from them again. 'I don't think she wants to talk to us. I think she wants us to go away. We'll just have to retrace our steps and go around, above the valley.'

Somewhere, deeper in the valley, there was a cracking of branches and a crash. A raven winged its way out of the darkness, turned and flapped high up above them to settle, looking in the same direction as the woman in white.

'What was *that*?' Cassie asked. 'Is somebody felling trees?'

A deep rumbling echoed from beyond the narrowed area and then the sound of more cracking and the disturbance of foliage.

'I think *something* is breaking branches, Cassie, something *big* and I think we should leave.'

The hairs on the back of Isobel's neck were beginning to stand on end with a sense of danger she had not felt at the sight of the glowing woman.

'But what *is* it, Isobel? I simply must know!'

Isobel glared at her. 'Cassie did you learn *nothing* from being nearly dragged down a well when you were a child? There are monsters in this world. When you encounter one, you stay away from it!'

Cassie ignored this, and instead grabbed her sister by the upper arms, eyes sparkling with excitement. 'Oh my goodness, Isobel! Do you remember Bry telling us about *La Blianche Danme*? The white lady who sometimes protects lost people, or walks beside them in the night? I think that's *her*. Perhaps she's here to protect us from whatever is further along the path.'

'Well then,' Isobel said firmly. 'Let us thank her *very* politely and be on our way – My Lady!' she called, 'It has been a pleasure, and we are most grateful to you for warning us of danger. We will bid you a very good afternoon and – *Cassie!*'

She shouted as Cassie finally released her hand and ran towards the woman in white. A dramatic shriek announced the arrival of Madame Auffroy. Their usually placid governess stood with her hands on her heart for a long moment, mouth gaping in horror at the glowing fae woman, before turning and fleeing with more speed than Isobel would have believed her capable of. Isobel threw her hands into the air with complete exasperation, and then followed after her sister who was now stood within reach of the woman in white.

'My Lady!' Cassie was saying to her with earnest eyes. 'If there is danger here, then I won't leave you alone to deal with it. Please, only tell me how to be of assistance!'

A roar echoed along the valley and Cassie took an involuntary step back. The woman in white looked unruffled and slightly amused. She looked at the two young women, then she spared a glance towards the ravens which were gathering in the branches of the trees behind them and sighed. Then she spoke in the loveliest voice the girls had ever heard.

'Thank you for your kind offer,' she said. 'I assure you I do not require any assistance. However,' she looked at Isobel, 'you must find another path. Something has awoken *Lé Barbou.*'

'What's a barbou?' Cassie's eyes were wide with fascination, and she shrugged off Isobel's attempts to pull her away.

'He is something akin to an ogre, or troll. He is large, foul-tempered and very dangerous.'

'Thank you so much, My Lady!' Isobel said, pulling Cassie's wrist. 'We will do as you kindly suggest, and find another way home. *Cassie!* Come along now.'

Cassie fought to stay where she was, saying. 'We live at the castle. We're the mapmaker's daughters, Cassie and Isobel. We can fetch some of the soldiers to deal with the monster.'

'That will not be necessary. I bid you good evening, Cassie and Isobel.' She walked away, stepping lightly where the path dropped off, and turned out of sight around the jagged edge of a cliff that jutted from the steep valley.

'I have to see,' Cassie whispered. 'Isobel please, this is *magic*, a fée queen and a monster! How often does one get a chance in life to see such things?'

'I see magical creatures *far more often* than I care to apparently,' Isobel hissed furiously.

'Isobel please! Just a glance?' Tears sparkled in Cassie's eyes.

'If I let you have *one* look, will you *promise* to run away immediately after?'

'Yes! Isobel, I *promise!*'

They tiptoed swiftly to where the path dropped away sharply. Carrie lifted her hem and hopped down in two jumps, then turned and raised her hand to help Isobel.

'Come on, Issy! One look! You'll regret it if you don't, you know you will.'

Isobel hesitated, then quickly took Cassie's hand and dropped down beside her sister. They kept to the side of the path, crouching low, trying to see past overhanging branches to catch a sight of *Lé Barbou* in the gloom.

The White Lady was glowing like summer sunlight as she walked, without fear, towards the approaching sounds of rage and destruction. Foliage shook and cracked, and a huge branch spun end over end towards the White Lady. She sidestepped gracefully and it spun past her, ruffling the long curls of her hair. The branch crashed into the rocky hillside. Rocks and earth showered down and a stone the size of Isobel's head thudded onto the path. *La Blianche Femme* continued walking forward.

Isobel glanced at Cassie and saw her sister's hands were over her mouth.

'It's not safe. We should go,' Isobel whispered.

'I just want to see it!'

La Blianche Danme stopped walking when a roar sounded. Crashes, rhythmic thuds, that Isobel realised were running steps vibrated the trees. A tree trunk was thrust to a crooked angle with the shove of a huge arm, and Isobel saw it.

The ogre-like monster was twice as tall as the White Lady, haggard as a madman, with large feet and hands. It had a beard and ragged hair, a wide mouth, gaping with yellow teeth and a brutish jutting jaw. *Lé Barbou* was so covered with dirt and tangled with ivy that it almost blended with the shadowed woodland.

Its eyes were small and furious. It ripped a sapling out of the ground and swung with mindless fury at the White Lady. She leapt back with the elegance of a dancer and raised her hands palms up. Green shoots exploded from the earth and crawled like living things over the ground. Brambles and briars twisted around trees like snakes hissing with the rustling of their sprouting green leaves and thorns. White roses and bramble blossoms bloomed and, as *Le Barbou* raised a fist, green vines tangled around his wrist.

He roared in fury as his blow was snared. He pulled and fought where he was caught. White petals showered as he shook like a wet dog to try and free himself. *Lé Barbou* aimed a kick at the White Lady and she flicked her fingers. Briars snaked around his opposite ankle and dragged him from his feet as if he had stepped into a trap. He fell with a crash and a roar and fought to get up again, tearing at the tangled briars. Some held, and some snapped.

He fought along the ground towards her, and the briars dragged him back. Isobel realised she was entranced. She shook off her fascination and grabbed Cassie by the wrist.

'Time to go!' Isobel said firmly.

'But Isobel!'

'You promised!' Isobel grabbed Cassie by the shoulders and stared into her eyes until Cassie nodded. Then she dragged her sister away by the hand.

They both glanced back as they sneaked off, seeing the earth under the trees come alive with fresh green shoots. White roses grew and climbed. They arched above the path as the girls retreated, buds formed in seconds and then bloomed into perfect flowers. Some showered rose petals and turned into red rosehips and others rained pale bramble flower petals and ripened into rich shining blackberries.

'Cassie!' Isobel exclaimed as her sister plucked a blackberry and popped it into her mouth. 'Don't eat faery fruit!'

They climbed up the jutting rocks onto the higher level of the path and came eye to eye with a raven on a low-hanging branch. It watched them fearlessly as they walked past. Isobel grimaced and pulled Cassie away from it. The large black birds seemed to be gathering in the trees and flying high above, curious about what was taking place in the valley.

Cassie and Isobel hurried back along the path.

'Do you think she'll defeat him?' Cassie gasped. 'Did you see what she did?'

'She wasn't even a little bit afraid, Cassie,' Isobel assured her. 'She's far too powerful, but that monster was throwing trees. You or I might be killed before she could save us. She wanted to protect us, and she told us to go. So, we mustn't defy her or she'd be angry, do you see?'

'Yes! You're right. She didn't want us to be hurt! Oh my goodness! Just wait until we tell Flynn and Bry that we saw the White Lady. Wait!'

'What?' Isobel slid to a halt as Cassie stopped and sighed.

'We should have picked one of her roses to keep!'

There was a cry from ahead and they saw Madame Auffroy waving her arms, urging them on faster.

'Didn't father employ her to *protect* us?' Cassie laughed.

'To protect us from amorous gentlemen, Cassie, not ogres.'

'She didn't even see *Lé Barbou*, Isobel. She ran away at the sight of a woman who glittered.'

'I don't think she expected to have to protect us from a fée queen either!'

'Allez! Allez!' Madame Auffroy was shouting. Her hands were trembling. She didn't wait for the girls to arrive before setting off up the path that led towards the coast. A stream of muttered, unintelligible French drifted back to the girls until Cassie began to laugh. Madame Auffroy pulled up short then and turned. She began to shout, jabbing her shaking finger at Cassie. Her lips were white with fury and fear. Then she sat down on a tree stump. Covering her face with her hands, she began to cry.

'I didn't catch a word of what she said,' Cassie whispered, as she leant against a tree. 'I don't know why she was talking so fast. She knows my French is awful.'

Isobel was looking at their governess thoughtfully. 'She said it was the White Lady.'

'Well yes.' Cassie wrinkled her nose. 'But we knew that.'

Isobel nodded. 'She said the White Lady is known in France. She described her differently though.'

'Well, what did she say? The White Lady saved us. If she hadn't been there, if we'd walked down that path… She is one of the *good* fée. A princess of light and flowers.' Cassie's eyes were still bright with excitement.

'Yes. I believe that too but...'

'I won't hear a word said against her by Madame Auffroy,' Cassie said defiantly. 'She didn't see what we saw. She doesn't know what we know.'

'Very well,' Isobel nodded and turned. 'Then I shan't repeat it.'

'Wait!' Cassie said, 'What *did* she say? Why is she so *scared*?'

'She said that in France, and in England, it is known that the White Lady is a goddess of death,' Isobel spoke hesitantly. 'The goddess of a *"peaceful"* death is what she said precisely.'

'I don't understand. What does that mean?' Cassie stared at Madame Auffroy.

'Perhaps it's not the same legend,' Isobel shrugged.

'But a *peaceful* death...?' Cassie asked. 'Surely a peaceful death is a good thing?'

'*Death is death*,' Madame Auffroy shouted at them in heavily accented English.

She stood, unsteadily, wiping tears away, and carried on up the path.

'It's getting dark,' Isobel said quietly.

The sisters stood a moment. They looked back down the path, where the roaring of *Lé Barbou* had fallen silent. Then they followed after their governess.

SHAPESHIFTERS

And his eyes have all the seeming of a demon's that is dreaming,
And the lamp-light o'er him streaming throws his shadow on
the floor

Edgar Allan Poe

As the human girls at last ran back down the path, *La Blianche Femme* used fresh shoots of green brambles and briars to wrap *Lé Barbou's* ogreous limbs so that he could not attack her.

He ripped at the vines as they confined him, green ropes that twisted around his ankles and wound around his arms. She didn't use thorny briars of mature wood for fear that he would continue to fight and hurt himself on branches of ragged thorns.

He stumbled to his knees again and roared in rage as one of his arms was bound to his side.

Soon he became so entwined that he could barely move. The woman in white approached him. She ignored the roars and bellows of the furious barbou and touched a single glowing finger to his grubby forehead.

'Go back to sleep,' she said.

His red eyes closed, and his body fell limp. As she walked past him, the valley widened, and she stopped to look around. Nothing seemed out of place.

'What woke him up?' she wondered aloud.

A breeze swirled gently, stirring large rose petals on the ground around her in a circle, and lifting the tiny white petals from the blackberry flowers like snowflakes. The White Lady knelt and rested her hands upon the ground. Beneath her fingers the earth turned green.

She ignored the shoots and seedlings that erupted at her touch and closed her eyes. She could feel their fresh life, but reached past them, to where the deep roots tangled into mycorrhizal networks. The trees were intertwined beneath the earth, communicating. She listened to a language that was slow and unconscious. Within the woodland of Rozel, something was unbalanced. The trees were troubled, and it had nothing to do with the furious ogre that had woken so suddenly in their midst. On the face of *Lé Barbou* she had noticed red welts, which hadn't been caused by her brambles and briars.

She stood and frowned. Foliage rustled as if a squirrel had jumped, but she could see no squirrel. There were no animals to be seen at all. Except for ravens, which she recognised as fée creatures, there were no birds either, and no twilight birdsong. The White Lady tilted her head back and stared at the canopy of leaves above.

'What am I looking for?' she whispered.

Black wings fluttered and flapped as more ravens swooped in and flew past her.

'May I possibly be of assistance?' a smooth voice asked.

She inhaled sharply and turned. She did not allow herself to look surprised, and she did not step back or cede ground to the man dressed all in black, who had appeared directly behind her.

He looked young, though she knew he was not. He was pale, with hair black as a raven's wing and eyes the colour of midnight.

'Lord Regent,' she said with stiff politeness. 'Must you always sneak up on me?'

The Regent put a hand to his chest, feigning hurt feelings. 'My Lady, I do not sneak. I emerge from the shadows, which is far more sinister and so entirely different.'

'Is it?' The White Lady raised an eyebrow.

'You appear concerned, *Blianche Danme*. I see you have been self-lessly assisting humans again. And this time, despite the agreements…'

'Yes,' the lady in white sighed with exasperation. '*Yes*, I spoke to the human girls. One of them was very young and determined to help. I wasn't about to allow two young women to be murdered by *Lé Barbou* on one of his erratic rampages.'

The Regent turned and looked at the sleeping monster.

'I wondered where that noisy brute had gone. You have him trussed up very nicely I see. Is he dead?'

'No, of course not. I put him back to sleep. I will take him through the stones at Faldouët and release him into our world.'

'Oh, really? Practically on my castle doorstep? How *very* kind of you.'

'You are welcome, Lord Regent. Does your sudden appearance here indicate that I have overstepped into your territory?'

'Not at all,' the Regent smiled sweetly. 'It is a pleasant surprise to find you lighting up my dark woods.'

He held out a pale hand so that the illumination from her skin lit his fingertips.

'You are very charming this evening, Regent,' The White Lady said, stepping away. 'Yet, are you not here to condemn me?'

She stared at him defiantly, and the Regent looked taken aback.

'No. I am only curious why you work so hard to save humans from our kind.'

She waved a dismissive hand, 'You, who hate humans so much, could never understand.'

'They're not interesting enough to hate. I merely loathe them.'

'Really? You loathe them? Yet, I hear such strange stories attributed to you.'

'Oh really? I do love stories. Especially stories about myself. Tell me one, my Lady, and I will help you find whatever it is that you are looking for.'

The White Lady smiled. 'Very well...' She spoke as they strolled. 'Once upon a time an old lady was walking home and as she passed through a crossroads, she heard the plaintive meow of a tiny kitten. She picked up the little creature, which seemed almost new-born, and looked around. There were no houses it could have come from. Being a kind old woman, she decided to take the creature home with her to keep it safe and started on her way with the kitten in the crook of her arm.

'As she walked, she thought perhaps the kitten was not as young and small as she had initially believed, and before long she was confused to realise that it now seemed half grown. The further she walked, the larger it grew, becoming a full-grown cat almost as she watched. When the old woman realised that the cat was not a natural creature, she became afraid and decided to set it down. She was frightened to find that she could not put it on the ground. Her arms would not unfold, and the cat seemed settled against her chest.

'She walked on, in a state of some fear, and was horrified to find that the cat was still growing beyond a reasonable size. It was soon the largest cat she had ever encountered. Still it grew, as big as a dog and just as heavy, but all she could do was stagger on under its weight. The cat became so huge that each step was a struggle, but when she stumbled and staggered backwards a few steps, she thought for a moment it seemed lighter. This set her to thinking. Since the cat had been growing while she walked away from the crossroads, perhaps it would become smaller if she started to walk back. And so it was: with each step on the return journey, the cat became smaller and lighter, and soon she was rushing back to the spot where she had picked the kitten up. This time, when she tried to put it down, she was able to move her arms and set the creature down in the exact place that she had picked it up. Leaving the… *unpleasant* thing where she had found it, she was able to return home.'

The Regent laughed. 'What a strange little tale. I take it cats do not *usually* grow and shrink in the manner that you have described? I have little experience with them myself.'

'Cats do not ever do that, Lord Regent, as I am sure you are aware.'

'Ah! It must be some kind of *shapeshifting* creature then. A phooka perhaps?'

The White Lady looked at him and asked, 'Could a very old and powerful phooka ever turn itself into an entire flock of birds, do you think?'

The Regent smiled. 'Oh no, they most certainly could never do that. The kind of power and intellect and brilliance it would take to divide one's self and mind into multiple creatures is far beyond the capabilities of even the most accomplished phooka.'

'Is it? Then I wonder what manner of fée creature could do such a thing?'

'Do you?' The Regent tilted his head to the side. 'Do you wonder about it often?'

'No,' *La Blianche Danme* said coldly, then added, 'a similar story is told in Guernsey of a woman who picked up a small black puppy one night and found, as she made her way, that it slowly grew into a giant black dog.'

'Well that's hardly surprising.' The Regent waved a dismissive hand. 'Guernsey is quite infested with giant black dogs you know. What is one more, in the scheme of things?'

'Yes, there are far too many black dogs. It is a lovely island all the same. And *very* close… as the crow flies.'

The Regent laughed. 'Or as the raven flies? Certainly.'

'And just as in Jersey, they are always building churches. Once, centuries ago, you and I gathered many creatures of both our light and dark courts of fée and faîtchieaux. They all came together to prevent the desecration of our sacred ground when humans started to build a church upon it. Do you remember?'

'I do. I recall that it took days to dissuade the idiotic humans from building there. Very tedious.'

The White Lady glared at him.

'It was a feat of astonishing organisation and cooperation between us all to convince the humans to change their minds,' she narrowed her eyes. 'Would it surprise you to learn, that the same effect was achieved far more easily in Guernsey by a big black goat which appeared on the site of a proposed church and refused to leave?'

'I have a question.' The Regent raised a finger. 'Was it a big black goat? Or a *very* big black goat?'

'I am told it was ludicrously huge. An unnecessarily large goat. It remained at the proposed site of the church, smashing the building materials and carts and scaring horses away. It reappeared whenever building was to recommence, destroying things and chasing people, until a different site was chosen.'

The Regent folded his hands behind his back. 'Well, how convenient that such a wonderful creature appeared, and that the matter of the church was dealt with so efficiently. We should all be grateful to this goat I believe. And it managed it without ever once *speaking* to humans.'

'Oh, do you not speak to humans, my Lord?' the White Lady asked with feigned innocence. 'Because the people of these islands believe that a devil walks amongst them, you know.'

The Regent shrugged. 'Now why would they think something so foolish?'

'I imagine that it is because you and your *Tchéziot* companion match the description of what they call "The Devil and his Deputy". There are people who claim a prince of darkness appears to them. He offers them deals, or promises them riches, and then tricks them into absurd behaviour. They describe him as a handsome man with dark hair and dark clothing.'

The Regent held up a finger again and asked, 'One moment. Do they describe him as *handsome*, or as *very* handsome?'

The White Lady suppressed a laugh and continued speaking.

'When this so-called devil is having farmers dig up their fields, or their houses, searching for buried treasure, or promising them gold, and tying them up in riddles and impossible tasks... it seems he does *talk* to them.'

'Really? Well, I am quite forgetful sometimes. My thoughts are often... scattered.' He grinned. 'Perhaps we have both interacted with humans from time to time. What are a few broken accords between friends, after all?'

The White Lady stopped and turned. 'We are hardly *friends*, my Lord. So, what is it that you *want*, Regent?'

The man in black raised his brows at the open animosity in her voice.

'All I want is to be of assistance...' He tilted his head one way, and then the other, like a confused raven. 'Do you truly still consider me an enemy, after all these centuries of peace?'

They stared at each other. *La Blianche Danme* narrowed her eyes.

'Wherever I turn I see ravens and crows. You have eyes everywhere. You were never what I expected for a regent. And you have *changed*. I do not understand it, and I do not *trust* it.'

The Regent spread his hands. 'I promise I am not spying with sinister intentions, Lady. I simply wish to remain informed. I apologise if I have given you cause for suspicion. As for changing... It is in my nature, you know. One must adapt. If you think I am your enemy, Lady, why would you wander so close to my castle, in these wild woods at nightfall, all alone?'

The White Lady smiled. 'Alone? I am not alone.'

As the Regent glanced around dubiously, the White Lady made a little bow to a patch of ground covered in fallen blossoms. Petals stirred and then began to lift on a breeze, rising and gathering more petals, moving with a circular motion that lifted until it was chest height, forming a tiny whirlwind, which danced slowly in circles around the two fée folk.

'*Vielle D'Avoût,*' The Regent said with an expression of pleasure, 'I have heard of them. They are air sprites that infuriate human farmers by throwing all the hay around in the fields before it can be baled. Creatures of gentle, delightful chaos.'

He also bowed politely to the spinning petals.

'You do enjoy chaos, don't you? A *Vielle* or *Folle D'Avoût* is most often found dancing in fallen apple blossoms.'

'She is a pretty thing, but a *Vielle D'Avoût* is hardly the most intimidating companion.'

'Do you imagine that I *need* an intimidating companion, Regent? Well, now I have you, I suppose. Since you see so much, with so many eyes, please tell me… What is *wrong* in this place?'

The man in black jabbed a thumb over his shoulder at *Lé Barbou*.

'No, not *him*,' The White Lady said, 'There's something else. Something that woke him from years of sleep. Something that is bothering the trees.'

'It would have been pleasant if that mindless imbecile had slept for a few more decades. Pardon me, but did you say something is *bothering* the trees?'

'All things are connected. They are communicating that something is threatening these woods.'

The Regent looked around and nodded, 'I'm inclined to agree.'

'Are you? And why is that?'

The Regent compressed his lips as though he would avoid the question, then he spoke. His voice was tinged with annoyance as he admitted, 'Something has been killing my birds.'

'Killing *your* birds? Your ravens?' She put a hand to her lips to suppress laughter as she asked, 'What manner of creature would dare?'

The Regent grinned, 'You may well be amused, my Lady, but it is a most unpleasant sensation. Like having little pinches of oneself snuffed out unexpectedly. Whatever is doing it, is very fast and well hidden.'

'What do you see when it happens? What do your birds see?'

'Nothing.'

'Nothing at all?'

The Regent shrugged, 'A disturbance of twigs and leaves perhaps? No sign of any creature. Perhaps it is invisible.'

'Twigs and leaves … An invisible beast…' The White Lady looked with new eyes, turning, searching more closely.

'Twigs and leaves are rather *normal* within the woods of Rozel, *ma Blianche Femme*,' The Regent said dryly.

'Oh yes, but as we were just discussing, Raven Lord, things are not always as they appear to be. Some things merely seem to be what they are not. Some are invisible, some alter, some mimic, some hide in plain sight.'

The White Lady pointed to the leafy canopy high above, 'There! Something stirring the leaves, bending the lighter branches. I know what is happening, I think. They are particularly nasty creatures. I have seen them full grown, but I had almost forgotten they could seed.'

'Seed?'

'Spawn might be a better word.'

'I believe you are keeping me in deliberate suspense, Madame.'

She turned to him with a smile to meet his own, 'There is a type of creature unique to these islands known as *L'Êmânue*. The humans call them *the invisible monster* but in fact they're just very well disguised amongst the trees, with limbs like vines and branches. They grow to mimic their hosts. No wonder the trees are concerned. Sometimes *L'Êmânue* don't move for centuries, and they stunt and poison the trees they nest in. It is very rare that they ever meet and have offspring. Unfortunately, when they do, they have a great many. Like dandelions shedding seeds. The little ones take time to settle and at first they hunt like spiders.'

'How repulsive.'

She nodded. 'Perhaps they were biting *Lé Barbou* and that is what woke him. It is fortunate that we found them now, before they grow to the size of dogs and start attacking larger prey. When they infest the woods like this, they are known as *Les Mannes' á Fou*.'

'So now we know what we're looking for. Twig spiders.'

There was flapping as ravens that had been waiting in the shadows rose into the air.

'Careful Regent,' the White Lady said, placing a hand on his arm. 'When they are threatened, they tend to…'

She paused as she realised the Regent was looking at her hand on his arm, amused by the familiarity. Two of his ravens swooped down, carrying a whipping little creature that looked like a tangle of thin vines and leaves. It was shaped something like a squid, with a central body and a nasty little face. It was trying to entangle the ravens as they descended, wrapping its legs and arms around one raven's claws, lashing around the wing of the other.

Another raven swooped in from above. It snapped up the small monster in its beak, spat it onto the ground and pinned it as it landed, with sharp black claws against the white petals. The thing thrashed and chirped furiously.

'...Swarm,' The White Lady finished. 'When threatened, they tend to *swarm*.'

The woods came to life above and around them as spidery little bodies dropped from the canopy and leapt from the foliage. They skittered across the ground and launched themselves at the two fée from every direction.

The Regent shattered into a whirlwind of ravens that swirled around the White Lady like a shield. Birds began dropping from the air like heavy black rain, entangled with little monsters, each in its own separate battle. The White Lady raised her arms. Light blazed from her skin illuminating the woodland. Brambles and briars burst from the ground, lashing and tangling with *Les Mannes' à Fou* until the clearing was a seething mass of writhing foliage, black wings and swirling white petals.

'Absolute chaos,' said the Regent with delight as he reformed in a flutter beside *La Blianche Danme*. He plucked a little monster from the air as it jumped for his face and tossed it upwards for a swooping Raven to catch.

'I'm glad you're having such a delightful time, my Lord,' The White Lady said. 'Whatever shall we do with these creatures?'

'Let's tangle them all up in a big ball of vines, like a green prison. Then we can roll them up to Faldouët Dolmen. In this world they'll be a menace. In our world they'll be fodder for all the far nastier things that live in the dark woods. *Les Grignolles dé la Niet* will make short work of them.'

'Very well,' *La Blianche Danme* nodded. 'Draw in your birds, Lord Regent. Let *La Folle D'Avoût* pull them towards us.'

The Regent nodded agreeably. As the White Lady's briars twined around the struggling little monsters, his Ravens swooped back, diving into his chest and merging without impact, dropping *L'Emanue* spawn as they arrived. Injured birds hopped and flapped back to him. Dead birds dissipated as dark smoke. A tangled cage of briars and brambles wove together around the Regent and the Lady. The swirling breeze roared into a fearsome wind, and the Regent lifted a hand to protect his eyes, as the whirlwind turned into a furious maelstrom. He and the White Lady stood in the eye of the storm as everything else was lifted and dragged into the trap of brambles and briars. Above them little *L'Êmânues* spun helpless in the hurricane. Leaves were ripped from trees and white petals blurred with black feathers. The White Lady's hair swirled around her.

The last of *Les Mannes' à Fou* were pulled into the green cage that formed a wall all around them and the whirlwind slowed. White petals rained down on them like snow in the enclosed space.

The Regent looked around and smiled as petals began to settle upon their shoulders.

'Well, this has been very enjoyable.'

'Enjoyable?' The White Lady laughed. 'You found *this* enjoyable?'

'Yes,' the Regent nodded. 'And so did you. Don't pretend otherwise. You should certainly reconsider the matter of our friendship.'

DRAGONS

We looked down the wonderful wing-filled regions
Where the dragons darted in glimmering legions.
Vachel Lindsay

The most famous dragon of the Channel Islands was the green dragon of the St Lawrence marshes, also known as the Dragon of *La Hougue Bie*. She wreaked chaos upon Jersey but was not averse to paying visits to other islands with a few beats of her immense wings. Once there she would attack anyone who did not seek cover. She delighted in terrifying people, lighting up the sky with flame at night and shadowing the islands with her wings during the day so that she could watch people scurry and scream.

Her story is well known. Green dragons tend to be carelessly arrogant, especially ones as young as she was. After all, what do dragons have to fear, except other dragons? As green dragons grow centuries older and larger, their bodies develop the ability to breathe toxic fumes that cause their prey to fall unconscious, and that turn their flames a sickly yellow.

Almost all dragons breathe fire, but different-coloured dragons exhibit different habits and strengths. Only the great and rare red dragons grow to such a size that they can easily destroy or burn an entire city to the ground, but their immensity eventually becomes their weakness. It is hard for a giant old red dragon to continually find enough food to stay awake, and they often sleep centuries away waiting for areas to repopulate with enough animals to provide them with a decent meal.

Most dragons never grow to anywhere near the size of the reds, however.

Black dragons and white dragons are the smallest, and they grow the most slowly.

Black dragons live in the deep places, in caves and caverns far beneath the living world. They despise daylight, or light of any kind, and almost never breathe their fire, which is a virulent green flame. Instead, they spit acid and exhale poison gas. They are so toxic that a place where a black dragon lives begins to die. When they make their lairs under forest, the trees turn to white skeletons. Noxious vapours drift from the earth and standing water sickens those who drink it. Eventually animals will not venture into a black dragon's territory at all, and the dragon is forced to find a new lair where they can claw beneath the surface of the earth. When they emerge, they do so only at night.

It is only during the very coldest winters that white dragons of the Arctic fly far enough south to encounter humans at all. Their breath is cold enough to freeze a man so completely that a single blow will shatter him like broken glass. Dragons do prefer their meals warm, however, and polar bears are a white dragon's favourite prey.

The second most famous dragon of the Channel Islands was the blue dragon who attacked Guernsey on the thirtieth of December, 1671. He caused at least as much permanent destruction as his far more famous green cousin, but he never achieved the same fame. This was for the very simple reason that the dragon was only sighted by a single person, and his tale was considered a lie. Lee was a baker's boy of twelve years old, unable to sleep due to the bursts of hail rattling against the shutters of his windows in the early hours of the morning. He noticed little crackles of static electricity were suddenly popping on his hair and bedclothes as he tossed and turned, letting out snaps of light. He found himself suddenly very much awake and, despite the cold, he got out of his bed and threw open the shutters of his high attic window, to look over St Peter Port.

The clouded light of the moon reflected on the choppy waters of the harbour. Lee's attention was arrested by the unusual motion of the dark storm clouds. They were swiftly parting in much the same way as the sea will part before the prow of a ship, rolling back onto them-selves and churning away. This happened in first one direction, and then again, as another line cut across the sky. He could see the fading traces of similar lines, as though a spiderweb of air was being formed above Castle Cornet.

Lee later described that he felt his knees bend almost instinctively, ducking as something huge passed overhead. He felt a rush of air blow his fringe back from his forehead, scattering hailstones into his room. His fingers clenched against the window frame as his body went cold with nameless dread. His short hair lifted and stood on end. When he tried to pat his hair down, it crackled.

Feeling both afraid and rather stupid, Lee stayed crouched down, wondering whether he had imagined something passing above him. He squinted at the dark sky. When the shifting clouds above Castle Cornet began to pulse and part from a central dark core, he saw everything that was happening, and watched with bewildered interest.

Pale clouds swirled around the beating of vast, bat-shaped wings. Wings that slammed the air with the speed and noise of a huge, relaxed heart. The rich, dark membranes of the wings were subtly patterned with pale details, as though constellations of stars and swirling galaxies had been delicately painted upon them by nature. If the monster had glided against a clear night sky, it would have been nearly invisible. Its natural camouflage would hide it from prey or an enemy dragon as it lingered high in the darkness, waiting to dive and destroy. It made no effort at concealment as it moved to position itself above Castle Cornet. Its tail lashed as it moved lower. Its attitude reminded Lee of an angry cat. The huge creature – which Lee, not being at all a stupid boy, had realised was a blue dragon – started to glow from within. The light grew deep within its chest, as pale as ghost fire, illuminating the dragon in the darkness. Electricity rippled across the scales of the monster, lighting it up. The dragon had scales of a vibrant cobalt blue, richer than sapphires. Its wingspan was longer than any of the boats at anchor in the harbour below; even hovering near Castle Cornet's elegant towers, it looked huge.

The light in its chest grew until even the dragon's eyes were sparkling white. Then the dragon opened its jaws and spat. A jagged line, not of fire, but of purple lightning, flashed across the sky and struck true into the Castle.

It was a thunderbolt of wicked accuracy, so bright it imprinted itself on Lee's retinas, freezing the image of the dragon blasting the castle with lightning. He closed his eyes, which saved him from the worst of the blinding explosion that followed. The dragon strike ignited the incendiary materials in the castle armoury, which detonated with a force that blew Castle Cornet entirely in half, shearing the top away completely. The keep and the great hall disappeared in an instant. Seven people were killed, more injured. The Governor Lord Hatton woke up bewildered, with hail striking his face, to find his bed had been blown out of the castle onto the outer wall.

The percussive force of the explosion knocked Lee on his back and shook the house. The sound of the explosion was so great that it woke people in the other Channel Islands. The Guernsey population of St Peter Port awoke, half-deafened, scrambling in confused fear. Falling out of beds and screaming confused questions at each other. They imagined an attack from foreign soldiers, or that their houses were falling around their ears. They stumbled in terror from their homes to see the refigured shape of Castle Cornet distorted and ablaze.

Those who didn't rush away in their night-shirts to try and provide help stood astonished at the destruction that could be wrought by a single lightning bolt. Almost none took the time to wonder why the storm that must have caused it should have passed so swiftly, or why no rumbles of thunder should have woken anyone before the castle exploded. The sky was still churning and flickering, but the dragon was gone.

Lee tried to hold his father back from running to lend his aid. His father shook him off gently, explaining that Lee was being foolish. There were no such things as dragons that spat lightning – Lee must have had a nightmare.

Of those that Lee tried to tell afterwards, only the most generous assumed that he had been dreaming. Most muttered that the boy was making up stupid stories for attention. They all knew of the green dragon that had terrorised Jersey, but who ever heard of a *blue* dragon? And how, indeed, could a surely mindless beast like a dragon know how to hit the castle precisely where it would cause the most damage? Why would a dragon even want to blow up a castle?

Anyone familiar with the behaviour of dragons would have been able to explain, of course, that the very existence of a castle would be considered an affront to them. The suggestion, should it occur to those great beasts, that humans might imagine they could ever protect themselves from dragons, in any way at all, would be enough to cause them to immediately disprove the idea.

For Lee, watching the night skies with continued interest through his long life, dragons became his obsession.

Late nights are not helpful to a baker's son, dragged yawning from his bed before dawn, and Lee eventually became an innkeeper. This was a vocation that lent itself better to staying up late. He visited Paris and purchased the most expensive telescope he could afford. He shipped it carefully home and earned a reputation for himself as a stargazer. In truth he was watching the night skies for monsters.

It was a number of years before he saw another dragon. It was small and black as pitch against the moon. It was a brief glimpse that made his heart leap in his chest with fear and joy. He woke his patient wife, warning her they must be ready in case of attack, but nothing happened.

After that Lee began to see dragons more regularly, like some siren call had gone out that was drawing them to the islands. At first it filled him with as much terror as excitement. When no reports of destruction or death reached his ears Lee was relieved, and then confused. He realised then that while he saw dragons head towards the islands, winging their way inland, he never saw them leave.

Where could a dragon hide on an island? Where could *so many* dragons hide?

One brutal winter night Lee's wife insisted he should stay in bed, despite the fact that his snoring made his frequent absences a private mercy to her. He laughed and promised he would only sit and watch until his nose turned numb. That was the night he saw a flight of white dragons, pale as ghosts.

He was well into his sixties, his eyesight fading, when he saw the red dragon.

It was a rich scarlet, the colour of blood, and it glided in as the sun began to rise. Its scales were lit up like flames and its huge wingspan dragged a purple shadow across the island as it descended.

Refusing to believe that such a vast monster could land in Guernsey without leaving some sign of its arrival, Lee put on his boots and set out in the direction he had seen it descend.

He threw on a coat and walked North towards L'Ancresse, where he believed the dragon must have landed. It was a place most islanders avoided.

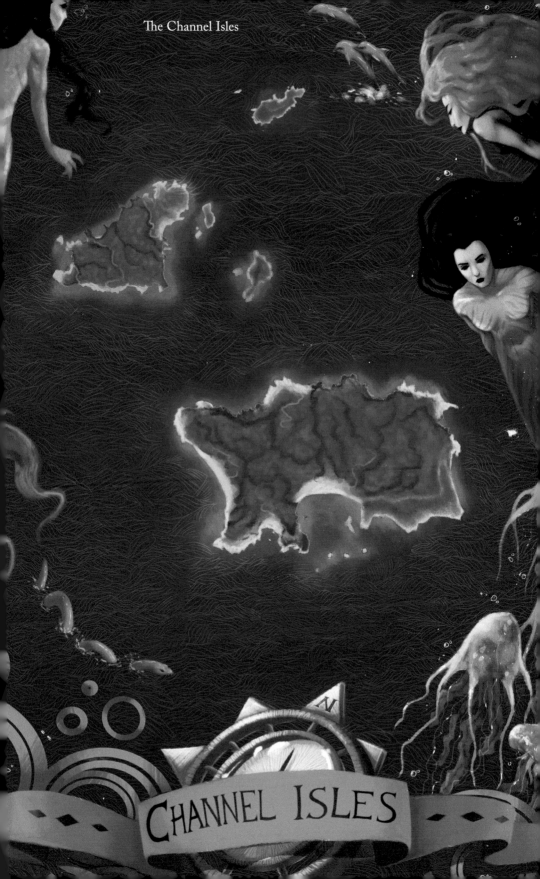

CHANNEL ISLES

La Cocangne

The Mermaid

Black Dogs

L'Êmânue

La Vioge

Hearth Faeries

La Blianche Danme

Shapeshifters

Lé Bélengi

Les P'tits Faitchieaux

Lé Croque-Mitaine

Revenants

Les Syraines

Storm Witches

Les Loups Garous

Dolmen stones littered the area, and the superstitious spoke of the land being sacred to the fée. The land had few features, save for standing stones and gorse. There was nothing that could conceal a creature of the red dragon's immense size.

Disappointed, Lee walked without expecting to find anything.

It was chance that caused Lee to notice the great gouges in the land – he simply tripped over one. He backed away to look at the lines of fresh, dark earth. They were almost like furrows cut by a plough. He climbed up upon a little rise and regarded the scoring of the ground. He could see it in his mind's eye, huge claws scarring the earth as the dragon landed. The back claws, he realised, and jumped down to find the compressions of the front claws. He found flattened ground and holes he could fit his foot in, the punctures of great talons, where the dragon had settled, and its weight had crushed the soft grass.

He was exhilarated, then for a moment he remembered what he was looking for and panicked, looking around wildly. The creature had certainly landed here yet it was nowhere to be seen now.

'Where did you go?' Lee wondered aloud.

He could see where it had stepped, just a few prints, then there was nothing.

Lee sighed in frustration and shrugged. He was about to seat himself beside a dolmen to rest and consider the matter, but hesitated when he noticed the smears of mud on the closest stone. The dragon had touched or clawed at it for some reason, but the stone did not appear to have been moved.

Lee stepped back from the stone as a tickle of fear ran from his neck down his back. For a moment he reconsidered the legend that the dolmens were Pouquelaye, Faery Stones, where Goblins danced and sly creatures stole away children. Only the most superstitious people believed such things.

Lee raised his hand to touch the stone. Then he pulled his fingers back.

Curiosity will only take a man so far. Lee knew he had a good life, and a good wife, and that dragons are certainly best seen from a distance.

Perhaps, he decided, it was wiser not to try to follow wherever they had gone.

With a little nod, Lee turned and walked for home.

LE BÉLÉNGI

Now through the dark old haunted mill,
So eerily, so eerily,
He flits, and with a whippoorwill
Mouth calls, and seems to syllable,
'Come follow me! Come follow me!'

Madison Julius Cawein

There were those who believed that the famous green dragon of Jersey was attracted to the islands, not because they were undefended, or even because the cattle were so well-fatted and so plentiful, but because the St Lawrence marshes in Jersey stank of gold.

The reason some of the locals held this belief was because of another creature, who had lived within the marshes for far longer: *Le Béléngi*. There are at least two béléngi in the Channel Islands, one in Jersey, and another in Guernsey. Both of the béléngi could at first glance be mistaken for a Will-o'-the-Wisp, those common creatures of the British and Irish marshlands, floating blue lights that drifted away at the approach of humans. Wisps always stay ahead and out of reach of those who pursue them. People often mistake them for the safety of lantern light when they are lost in the darkness, where one false step might cause a man to slip and fall into neck-deep water or clinging mud. They fade in the presence of light, retreating into shadows. Yet in darkness they glow an eerie blue and move like living things.

Wisps are often explained away as faerie-fire, a natural phenomenon of blue flames that feed on marsh gasses. Yet no one is certain why, no matter which direction they are approached from, or how carefully they are tracked, wisps drift away and can never be reached.

In Jersey it was said that the béléngi of the marshes protected a great treasure, consisting of gold in vast quantities, coins or ancient chalices and masses of tangled jewellery. Some people believed that if a person could follow the flickering blue light long enough, they might be led to the exact spot where the béléngi hid this fortune. For some people this was such a feverish conviction that they would go out into the marshes and dig at random, hoping that the edge of their shovel might one day strike something hard and bright. They were always disappointed. No human can sniff out gold.

Dragons, on the other hand, can smell gold from leagues away. They like to line their nests with it. They measure the greatness of their lair by the shining amassed wealth of the soft metal.

After the initial terror occasioned by the green dragon's arrival some of the experienced treasure hunters began to wonder ... had the green dragon located the béléngi's gold? Was she even now settled and sleeping on the very site where the treasure was hidden? Why else would a dragon choose to live in such a wet and inhospitable place as the St Lawrence Marshes? A béléngi was invisible during the day; a huge green dragon most assuredly was not. So, if it was sleeping where there was treasure...

This idea became too much for one husband and wife who had spent much of their deeply unhappy marriage digging in the marshes in locations where they had sighted the béléngi. Years of leaking boots, damp socks and disappointment had done little for their marital harmony, but they refused to give up. They decided to try and sneak into the marshes and watch, from a safe distance, where the green dragon was sleeping. When the husband and wife did not return, it was remarked by their neighbours that the dragon, just like anybody else, most likely enjoyed an unexpected meal delivered to its home.

Another treasure hunter, not put off by the fate of the husband and wife, but planning to avoid the dragon, set out one night to search for the elusive béléngi. He was only half an hour into his careful slog, through knee high water and banks of reeds, when he heard the dragon roar. He dropped to a crouch. In the distance the sky lit up with orange flame, and he glimpsed the silhouette of the dragon rearing, her wings spread. When her flames faded he saw her silhouette lit with vivid blue light and heard her roar in rage and pain.

For years he had hunted the béléngi, stumbling into mud and being bitten by flying insects. He had followed it in circles many times, had nearly drowned on more than one occasion as it led him to unexpected deep pools of water.

He had never been afraid of it before.

The next day he packed up his things and booked passage to France. He warned other treasure hunters that, whatever the béléngi was, it was not a wisp. Anything that could make a dragon roar was not going to be troubled by a man with a shovel.

'Even if there is treasure,' he said, 'nobody's getting anywhere near it.'

The Guernsey Wisp is different from its Jersey counterpart, and from Wisps in general, because it does not make its home in swamps or marshland. The Guernsey *Faeu Bélenger* is only encountered upon the beaches of the north-east coast, most often between Vale Castle and Houmet Paradis. It only appears on nights that are foggy or when the sea mists drift in like an army of ghosts. For many years the floating blue light of the bélenger itself was mistaken for the lantern of a wandering ghost. There were even those who believed the blue wisp of Guernsey was the great, glowing single eye of a huge half-blinded sea serpent that feasted on the bodies of drowned sailors when they washed ashore.

As with anything unexplained or mysterious it attracted the curious and unwary. When legends of the béléngi's treasure in Jersey carried across the sea, some people began to wonder if there was also treasure in Guernsey. Perhaps the ghost-light marked the shipwrecked bounty of ancient barques buried under the sand. Maybe a flickering fée light marked the path back to an ancient faery hoard.

There were always people who, despite their knowledge of the treacherous island tides, would see a strange blue light illuminating the fog and set out to find it. The bélenger always seemed to be just out of reach, masked by the cool veils of sea mist. Treasure hunters would walk swiftly across the sand, stumbling over rocks, slipping on seaweed, certain that just a few more steps might reveal treasure. Sometimes they wandered in circles as the bélenger drifted. When men splashed into the shallows of the turning tide, they tried to turn back, their curiosity unsatisfied. Then they would find that they had wandered behind labyrinthine walls of jagged rock, with waves whispering over the sand to cut off their retreat. Lost in the dark, they would panic, climbing over rocks, swimming or floundering in a rising sea. They became turned around in a world of pale mist, realising they no longer knew which direction was land and which was sea. Some made it back, wet and afraid, to tell their tales of warning. Some people, as is always the way for those living close to the ocean, simply disappeared.

William was fascinated by the legends of the bélenger. When he was very young, he had seen it drifting high on the beach, near where his family lived. Over the years the tales he heard caused him to develop a fixation with it. Even at the age of fifteen he would still watch from his bedroom window, especially on misty nights, and whenever there was fog. He would stare out at the beach until his younger siblings teased him for it. They had long ago lost interest in accompanying him out on foggy nights to walk around in darkness and disorientation, in the hope that some faint blue light might appear. Therefore, it was with irritated surprise that Marcus, William's younger brother, found himself being shaken awake one February night from a deep sleep. He was half-dragged from his bed to the window, where it took some time for his bleary gaze to focus on a soft blue glow lighting the wet sand in the distance. There was enough mist to distort the glow, but he could see that it emanated from a single point, moving by the tide line.

'Get dressed,' William whispered loud in his ear.

Marcus's protests were enough to wake their sister Daisy, who pushed open the door to their room and hissed angrily for them to shut up.

Daisy, on having the bélenger pointed out to her, immediately ran back to her room to get dressed and find a lantern. Marcus, not wishing to seem cautious where his sister was bold, irritably put back on the clothes that he had left lying on the floor at bedtime.

'We should take a shovel in case it marks the path to a faery treasure!' William almost dragged his brother down the stairs and outside, while Daisy, struggling to get her coat on, called softly for them to wait for her.

By the time William and Marcus had found the garden shovel in the shed, Daisy was already trotting for the beach. The lantern light was bobbing with her every step, and the boys ran to catch up to her.

'Put that wretched thing out, it's making me night blind – I can't see a thing. We'll lose it!' William berated her quietly.

'Why are you whispering?' she asked loudly. 'Nobody can hear us now. I'll put it out when we get closer.'

'Be quiet! What if you scare it? Put the lantern out *now*.'

'I'll put it out when we get onto the sand. We're not going to find your precious *Faeu Bélenger* if one of us trips over and breaks a leg trying to run about in the dark. You're so *stupid*, Will.'

They bickered until they reached the flat sand, Marcus insisting that if William wanted a shovel then he should be the one to carry it. For a few moments after Daisy shuttered the lantern, they thought William was right and they had lost the bélenger. Then their eyes adjusted and the faint blue glow became visible again.

'Come on!' William set off at a run, his silhouette black against the faint cerulean glow, the shovel held across his chest.

With exclamations of annoyance and complaint, Marcus and Daisy began to jog after him. Daisy was slowed by the heavy lantern. She had no wish to break the glass and incur their parents' anger, so she set it carefully on the sand and left its comforting yellow light behind as she raced after her brothers. The silhouettes of the two boys seemed to run upon nothing but diffused blue light as they raced into heavy mist. Soon Daisy could barely see where she was setting her own feet. She was more certain with every step that she didn't really care what the ball of blue light was.

She slowed and spared a glance back to where the warm, shuttered glow of the lantern was still just visible. As she hesitated, there was a deep blue flash and a cracking sound like a branch snapping. A jagged scrawl of lightning tore the night. The shovel that William had been carrying was lit up as it lifted into the air and then dropped with a slap onto the wet sand.

Then the world went black.

'Daisy get the lantern!' Marcus's scream was hoarse with terror.

Daisy, lost in suffocating black sea fog, did not need to be told twice. She raced for the lantern, sprinting far faster back towards its weak light than she had towards the bélenger. She opened the lantern shutters, and let it blaze, but it made little difference. Everywhere mist reflected the light. She might as well have been looking inside a cloud for her brothers. It was only Marcus's voice that led her on as he shouted for her help. Then suddenly he was looming out of the mist to take the lantern and running to kneel down where William was lying on the sand.

'Help him sit up!' Daisy cried.

'I can't,' Marcus's face was ghostly white. 'He's hurt, Daisy. He's burned. It was like lightning hit him, it threw him back past me, and–'

Daisy pushed Marcus aside impatiently, 'It's alright, William,' she said gently. 'Everything will be fine. You'll be fine.'

She dropped to her knees beside him, moving the lantern closer. One side of William's face was livid red and he was breathing erratically. His clothes were blackened and scorched.

'We need to help him home,' Marcus said. 'The bélenger could still be out there, Daisy, but I don't know how to move him without hurting him.'

William grabbed Daisy's wrist, his eyes wild, and tried to say something. She leant forward so she could make out his faint whisper.

'What's he saying?' Marcus asked.

William's hand released her, fell limp onto the wet sand, and his body became still. Daisy began to cry as Marcus checked for William's pulse. She saw his face twist with misery, then her little brother's arms enclosed her in a fierce hug.

'We'll have to go and get Dad,' Marcus said. 'We can't carry his body, Daisy. We need to leave him. Just for now. Please, it's not safe here and I'm not losing you too. *Come on!*' He pulled her to her feet and picked up the lantern.

They began to walk, holding hands, like something might otherwise snatch one of them away into the darkness. With no other idea of their bearings, they followed their own footprints back through the pall of sea mist.

'What was it?' Daisy asked, 'The bélenger. What did it look like?'

'I don't know,' Marcus shook his head. 'I couldn't see. Will was too far ahead of me. It just looked like a ball of flickering blue light. Will ran right at it as fast as he could. Then there was a flash, and he was suddenly up in the air like he'd been thrown. Then everything went dark. What did he say to you?'

Daisy sniffed and wiped her tears. 'He said, *"Behind the light."* That's all he said, *"Behind the light."*'

'What does that mean?' Marcus asked.

'I don't know.'

They exchanged glances, the tracks of their tears glistening in the lamplight, and hastened their steps towards home.

LES P'TITS FAÎTCHIEAUX

Some day you will be old enough to start reading fairytales again.

C.S. Lewis

The sound of the front door opening and closing made Charles smile and lower his book.

'Constance Lestienne has gone mad,' Laurence shouted from downstairs.

'With love for you again?' Charles called back. 'What have I told you about being so damn charming?'

He set aside the book and trotted down the stairs with a swift ease that belied his years. He found his companion in the kitchen. Both men were nearly in their sixties but neither showed their age. Laurence, especially, with his fine bone structure and the bright smile that he was now directing at Charles, was a man of striking good looks.

'No, Charlie,' Laurence leaned on the table. 'Not with love for me. Although I had to hear the usual nonsense about what a terrible waste it is for two men like us to be living unmarried, sharing a house, with nobody to take care of us, if you please – like neither of us knows how to wash a dish! She mentioned how tall and handsome you are, Charlie, *despite* your red hair.' Laurence's blue eyes danced with amusement. 'Perhaps she's changing tack? Ready to settle for a second choice?'

'Bless her dear lonely heart, but my dance card is entirely full. Does this mean neither of us will be safe shopping for groceries in peace? Good grief.' Charles gestured at the baskets of groceries on the table and floor. 'How did you carry all of this?'

Laurence flexed his tanned hands. 'Slowly and carefully and I took a little rest halfway home. The larder is getting a little sparse, and she had such wonderful fruit for this time of year. Look at these persimmons!'

'What on earth is a persimmon? It looks like an orange tomato. Wait! Stop distracting me with strange fruit. Why has Constance Lestienne gone mad, Laurie?'

Laurence carefully set paper bags full of fruit on the table and paused dramatically with one hand in the air.

'Wait until you hear this, Charlie. She's closing the shop early, before it gets dark, because of the excavation work at the La Hougue Bie site. One of the archaeologists told her they've found an entrance to the dolmen. She believes they're going to accidentally release a particular type of faery. I can't remember what she called them. It will come to me. Let's have a cup of tea, shall we? I am emotionally drained. Constance practically herded me around the shop, flapping her hands at me, telling me she needed to shut everything up and get home before it gets dark.'

'Faeries? She's scared of faeries in 1924?' Charles shook his head as he filled the kettle. 'I knew people were still superstitious in these islands, but that's quite something. Imagine being afraid of a couple of little faeries digging their way out of a neolithic site.' He put the kettle on the stove and began to help put the food away as Laurence continued.

'It's not just a couple of faeries apparently. Oh! I remember what she called them! The Shadows of the Night. "*Les Grîngnolles dé la Niet,*" in the Jersey-French. The sort of faeries people believe in over here aren't pretty little butterfly things, Charles. It's a serious business.'

'It may well be, but I spent my formative years away at Oxford and in the military, Laurie. I missed out a bit on all the local fairytales.'

'Oh, did you go to Oxford, Major?' Laurence paused with a box of eggs and raised his eyebrows, 'You only mention it two or three times a week these days, so I almost forgot.'

They grinned at each other for a moment before Charles laughed.

'Go on then, what type of faery is Constance expecting to explode from this dolmen when the sun finishes going down? A military man should always be prepared, and we only have a few minutes. It's dusk. Good grief I wish this house had electricity. We should light a lantern.'

Laurence sighed dramatically. 'I know, I know, when you were in London the nights fairly blazed with light. It must be such a terrible hardship to be stuck here with me in the dark ages, with lanterns, and dolmens and fairytales.'

'And yet, somehow, I am *perfectly* happy. What type of faeries are these 'Shadows of the Night'? They don't sound like something from a nursery rhyme.'

'I have to admit this is the first I've heard of them. Growing up people always talked about the dolmens and the standing stones being connected to *le fée* and *les faïtchieaux* and that you should stay away from them because they were doorways to faeryland. But *le fée* were the same size as us. Well, not you perhaps, you're far too tall. But normal human sized creatures. The legends have all kinds of faeries, big and small. It's no surprise I hadn't heard about them all. Anyway, it's not just Constance, it sounds like everybody in the neighbourhood is barricading themselves in tonight in case the wicked faeries come for them.' He waggled his fingers in mock terror.

The kettle began to whistle, and Charles took it off of the stove while Laurence rinsed the teapot and went on, 'There are some scary ones though. My mother used to tell me if I didn't make my bed in the morning the crooked faery would come for me. In retrospect she really was a dreadful parent.'

'You didn't make your bed in the mornings? Serves you right. Anybody who doesn't tuck down military corners should have to fight a little faery as a reminder.'

'Oh no, the crooked faery was tall and thin, twisted and evil, with long teeth and claws. He folded his limbs with cracking sounds. He hid under beds and ate children who were naughty. Or he bit their feet if they left them hanging out from under the covers. Something like that. The thought of it used to scare the life out of me.'

'Oh, you poor little thing! Yet clearly the threat didn't work, since you never do make the bed. Did you remember to buy milk, Laurie?'

'Yes. There's still half a bottle behind you though.'

'And these shadows of the night are like this crooked fellow, are they? Should I unpack my old Enfield?'

Laurence laughed. 'You can't kill faeries with rifles, Charlie. Iron's the thing you need. Sometimes silver works, I think… all the folklore muddles together in my brain. Good lord what is that noise? It sounds like there's paper blowing around everywhere. There wasn't a breath of wind on the way home.'

Laurence opened the kitchen window and leaned to look out, then walked down the short hall and opened the front door. Charles was about to pour the tea when he heard Laurence call his name.

'What is it?' he called back.

'Charlie come and look at this.'

Charles set the teapot down and walked swiftly down the hall. There was something in Laurence's voice that did not allow for hesitation. Laurence was standing just outside the front door, facing up and to the right, his brow knit, and his lips parted. Charles followed his gaze upwards to the darkening sky. To his poor eyesight it seemed that winding grey clouds of chimney smoke flowed back and forth like twisted veils against the fading colour of a dying sunset.

'Are those birds?' asked Laurence. 'Is it them making that noise?'

'I don't have my spectacles.'

'They're on your head, Charlie,' Laurence said without looking at him. 'They're always on your head.'

'So they are.' Charles slid his glasses on, took a few steps into the garden, and stared at the sky. The veils of darkness snapped into focus, and he saw the merging clouds were made up of thousands of tiny shapes, indistinguishable from this distance.

'Isn't it starlings that all merge together in great flocks like that? What do they call it, there's a word, *susurration* or something?' Laurence asked.

'A *murmuration* of starlings. Although I think both words apply here. That noise… like dry leaves whispering in the breeze. It's certainly them. Although I don't think they are starlings. I think they're bats. It must be bats. Look how fast they are! The way they're rising and gathering. Do you see they're all lifting from below the trees and joining the formation above. How do they all move so closely without touching? How very beautiful they are.'

They stood, mesmerised by the growing, spreading, dancing cloud of little flying creatures, until Laurence remarked, 'That's the direction of La Hougue Bie, isn't it?'

'It is.'

'Do you think the excavation disturbed some huge underground cavern of bats?'

'I do not.'

'Why not? Charlie? Why not?'

'Look at the gate-post.'

'Why, what's wrong with the…?' Laurence trailed off as he followed Charles's gaze.

A thing crouched, no taller than a handspan, skin dark with mud but cold grey under the dirt. Its long sharp fingers twitched and its wings rustled like old leaves. Its eyes were hard and black and coldly intelligent. When it smiled, its wide little mouth was full of sharp teeth.

'Who could imagine that Constance Lestienne would ever be right about something?' Laurence whispered.

'Iron, you said?'

'What?'

'Iron for fighting faeries.'

'I… yes, Charles, but do you think we *need* to fight him? He is *very* small.'

'It's all his friends in the trees behind that concern me.'

For a long moment Laurence couldn't see them. Then one moved, and his eyes adjusted to the shadows. Swift dark shapes crawled along branches. Hundreds of pairs of eyes glittered, all focused on the two men. Wings whispering like dry leaves.

'*Gringnolles dé la Niet,*' Laurence whispered.

'What do we have that's made of iron?' Charles asked again, his voice deliberately calm.

'I can't think… the skillet?'

'You get the skillet. I'll get the poker from the fireplace.'

'Do you think that if we back away slowly, that–'

'No, I think we should run. Run now, Laurence, get the skillet. I'll be right behind you.'

The second Laurence moved the faeries leapt. The air was filled with the sound of wings, and fear made Laurence fleet of foot. Charles leapt after him and slammed the door behind them, but some of the grîngnolles made it inside. Most of them hit the door with a sound like hard rain.

Charles ran across the parlour to the fireplace. As he grabbed the iron poker, Laurence shouted that the kitchen window was open. He was pulling it closed when Charles reached the kitchen. It had always been a stiff window, now it was jammed with fearless faeries forcing their way in. Laurence was trying to slow them by blocking the gap with the edge of the skillet and his hand. They were avoiding the pan, but they crawled and squeezed past Laurence's fingers.

Already grîngnolles were swirling in and out of the rooms of the house like sparrows. They swarmed over the newly filled fruit bowl, biting and clawing with their sharp little fingers. They were covering the loaf of bread in a mass of grey and devouring like locusts. The windowpane was now black with them, those behind were crushing those in front in an effort to get inside. Only those that were forced against the iron skillet hissed and flinched back.

Laurence yelped and recoiled, and there was blood on his fingers.

'Move, Laurie,' Charles jabbed with the poker, forcing a faerie back outside, swiped little bodies out of the way as best he could and slammed the sash down.

'One of them bit me!' Laurence was pale, skillet held to his chest, eyes on the fluttering little winged creatures darting around, growing in number.

Charles felt something sharp sting his cheek as one whipped past his face. The faerie landed, and hissed defiantly from the table, blood on its claws. Charles gently took the skillet from Laurence's trembling hands, raised it, and thumped it down with a crunch upon the little monster. He lifted the iron pan and watched in appalled fascination as the crushed creature wrenched and flexed its limbs and snapped back into shape. Where the skillet had touched its pale grey skin, it was a bit pink, as though the iron had been hot, but it showed no other damage. It flexed its claws and smiled.

'My god, they're like cockroaches.'

They lined the tops of the cupboards, looking down, more and more of them.

'Damn it, the study window is open upstairs,' Charles glanced at the little faces crushing against the glass of the kitchen window. It creaked in its frame. Their claws scratched against the glass. One of them began tapping, tapping with a little stone in its claws.

'The windows aren't going to hold anyway, Charles,' Laurence said quietly. 'There's too many, and when they finish eating the groceries… Charles, keep the skillet and hand me the poker.'

'Why the swap?'

'Because *you* are better at tennis, and *I* am the better fencer.'

'Yes,' said Charles handing Laurence the poker and touching fingers to the scratch on his face, 'But I don't think it's going to make any difference if they swarm. It galls me to retreat from such a small army, dear boy, but I'm afraid that you and I are going in the larder.'

'What?'

'Strong door. No windows. Plenty of provisions.'

'Yes! Good idea. "He who fights and runs away, may live to fight another day" and what have you.'

'"And he who is in battle slain can never rise and fight again" is the part everyone leaves out. Are you ready? I'll pull the door open. You jump in and I'll follow, quick as a wink.'

'Ready when you are, Major.'

They backed towards the larder door, shared a quick nod, and Charles wrenched the door open. Faeries sped towards them, but only three little monsters made it inside the enclosed dark space with them. Charles dealt with these while Laurence struck matches for him to see and occasionally lashed out with the poker. The larder was only twice the size of a wardrobe, making movement difficult. A jar of marmalade was shattered in the fray as Charles first batted the faeries down with the skillet, then grabbed and deposited them inside containers. Two were imprisoned in a half empty jar of pickles where they hammered their little hands against the thick glass. The third, Charles jammed in a large earthenware pot before wedging the cork in tight.

'Is that my jug of rumtopf?' Laurence demanded, outraged.

'Sorry, Laurie.'

'That rum cost a fortune, Charlie. I've been adding fruit to it for months, I was really looking forward to that.'

'I was too, dear boy, but it was the best thing to hand.'

'That faery is going to be absolutely legless by the time it gets out. Look there, Charlie, there's an empty tin you could have wedged it in! You hate rumtopf, don't you?'

Laurence held his match high just so that Charles could see his suspicious expression.

'A tin?' Charles shook his head vigorously before the match-light died, 'I couldn't put it in a tin. It would have been scratching against the metal all night, like a rat in a bucket, driving us both quite mad.'

The light began to fade, and Charles motioned that they should sit. He slid to the floor with his back against the door, setting the skillet aside with a dull clang. Opposite, Laurence hunched down and tried to get comfortable as they banged knees and eventually settled with their long legs half entangled.

'You think this will only last the night then, Charlie?' Laurence asked. There was a forced lightness to the question that made Charles think he was far more afraid than he was comfortable admitting to.

'Oh yes, it'll just be tonight. It's right there in the name, isn't it? The Shadows of the *Night*. Very dramatic but I'm sure they'll be gone when the sun rises. I dare say if we keep the windows shut for the next few evenings there'll be nothing much to worry about at all.'

'I think the word grîngnolles may actually translate to *nibblers*. It's not as dramatic, but it's certainly more accurate. My goodness, do you think the neighbour's cat will be okay?' Laurence asked.

'Spoopy? That fat thing!' Charles laughed. 'Probably already ate as many faeries as it could get its paws on. So… *The Nibblers of the Night*. What a very strange little siege we find ourselves in. I suppose it's a lot more comfortable than the trenches at any rate. Oh damn! I wish I'd thought to grab the corkscrew. We could have had a bottle of wine. Light a match will you, and I'll grab the cooking sherry. I could do with *something* to gather my nerves.'

'There's still a bit of good rum left. I bought two bottles. Not that you deserve any. Reach over by that rum topf that you've so heartlessly ruined, and it should be just behind.' He struck a match to aid in locating the bottle.

Charles grabbed it and passed it over, saying, 'Splash some on your hand, will you? Goodness only knows what kind of infection you could get from a faerie bite.'

Laurence's face twisted with sudden horror as the match flared and died. 'Oh no!' he whispered.

'Good grief, *what*?' Charles demanded, the horror in his companion's voice had filled him with dread. 'What's wrong? Are they poisonous or something?'

He grabbed for Laurence's hand in the darkness urgently, but Laurence only sighed, squeezed his fingers and said. 'No, Charlie. I just remembered I left a freshly baked Victoria sponge cake on the dining room table to surprise you. By now those little bastards will have savaged it. You have no idea how hard that was to carry home.'

'Oh for goodness sake, Laurence!' Charles grabbed for the rum bottle. 'Give that back. You scared me half to death.'

LÉ CROQUE-MITAINE

Something wicked this way comes.

William Shakespeare

'Are you going out again?' Iris heard the shrill note of panic in her own voice and wrung her hands as her parents exchanged glances.

'We'll only be gone an hour or so,' said her mother wrapping herself in a shawl.

'You always say that!' Iris could feel herself beginning to shout as they opened the door. 'You always say you'll only be an hour, and then you don't get home until after the pub closes!'

'For goodness' sake, Iris!' Her father stamped his feet into his boots. 'Stop shouting before you wake your sister! You're nearly eleven years old. It's time you grew out of your fear of the dark. We'll lock the door behind us, and you'll be fine.'

Her mother paused in the doorway to say. 'Mind what your sister says. And if we get home to find that you've lit every candle and lantern in the house again, you'll be in trouble, Iris.'

'If you need to get drunk,' Iris asked, 'why can't you just stay in and drink here?'

'Don't talk to your mother like that!' Her father closed the door only slightly less forcefully than a slam, and she heard the sound of a key turning in the lock.

The sun had already dipped beneath the horizon and the house was full of shadows as she ran up the hall and thundered furiously up the wooden stairs to the first floor and stamped across the landing to her room. She considered slamming her own door, but there seemed no likelihood of her parents hearing it. Instead, she ran to her window and slammed that shut instead. Outside the dying light was star-scattered indigo. Beneath the trees the world had already turned black.

'*Mind your sister*,' Iris mimicked her mother's instruction then muttered, 'How can I mind her when she's never here?'

Her older sister Katie would sneak out at all hours. When their mother and father tried to contain her she would climb out from her attic room, down over the stables and escape. Her friends lived only a short walk away in St Aubin's Village. Their parents never noticed, as long as Katie was home before they were.

Iris went to her dressing table and carefully removed the tall glass chimney-globe from her oil lamp. She struck a match and lit the wick. Then she replaced the glass globe and turned the flame up, full and bright. The oil lamp's heavy base reservoir was made of green glass so Iris could see that it was more than half full. She threw herself on her bed and refused to cry. The warm glow of the lamp was a comfort. The rest of the house was dark and silent. She had thought she would love this house when she was a little girl, although it was far too large for a family of four. It was three stories high, with an attached stable, and a dining room that could have sat twenty people. Her father had been a successful foreman when he bought the land overlooking a pretty little cove. His men had raised this house over the bones of the smaller, cosier cottage that he had torn down. The property had a mature orchard and was surrounded on three sides by woodland. It was within walking distance to the Portelet Inn, it had a private lane, and it was isolated and quiet. It was a beautiful home in a beautiful location.

Iris hated it.

Her room looked out over the shadowy, overgrown orchard. One of the trees was so near to her window that an adventurous girl could have easily climbed out into its closest branches, but Iris was not an adventurous girl. Iris was the sort of girl who never strayed from the path or went close to dolmens for fear that faeries would steal her away. She was frightened by stories of witches and werewolves, of goblins and ghouls, of fae creatures that could twist the thoughts and wills of normal people. She listened carefully when the children at school whispered about magic and monsters. Her parents laughed at her when she talked about something wicked in the woods. But Iris believed the stories completely. She believed because she had seen something, pale and stealthy, moving beneath the trees at dusk.

She never saw it clearly enough to be certain, but the glimpses were enough for her mind to spin nightmares of a tall thin man or a giant white spider. In her dreams the monster was both and yet neither. Iris thought she knew what was lurking in the darkness beneath the trees, and she was desperate to be wrong.

She watched the reflections of the lantern light shining in each of the little leaded panes of the window and could not help but wonder if it was out there now. *Lé Croque-Mitaine*, the crooked faery, out in the darkness, looking up at her light. She wished she'd remembered to close the outside shutters before slamming the window, but she could at least close the curtains. Iris almost moved to stand up, and then hesitated as she realised that she hadn't left the window open.

Of course she hadn't left the window open.

She never left the window open.

The window latch had always been a little bit loose. She had asked her father several times if he would fix it for her, but he had sighed, and said there were other, more important things on his list to deal with.

Her heart began to hammer. The fear became suffocating, like a weight on her chest that made it hard to breathe. Her palms were slick with cold sweat. Her senses heightened with terror, straining for any sound, and she noticed a smell, like damp earth and rot, and something more foul in the air, like the stink of a butcher's shop on a hot day. She knew, with sudden certainty and absolute clarity, that the monster was already in the house. Somewhere inside it was waiting, until just the right moment, savouring her fear. Her muscles tensed until she began to tremble, and a tear ran down her cheek, but she clenched her teeth determinedly.

Iris made a plan.

She would run. It was all she could do, really. The front door was locked, there was no easy way out, but there was nothing outside except darkness and the wild woods anyway. However, Iris knew her house well. She had watched it being built and remembered things about her home that other children might not have noticed. She knew exactly where to run to.

She took a shaky breath, and then threw herself from the bed towards the door, halfway across the room before her feet even touched the floorboards. She was fleet with fear and so she was nearly half-way across the landing, racing towards the shadowed stairs before she heard it behind her.

A glimpse showed her long arms clawing out from under her bed, and she knew it was the crooked faery. Something of its size could only fit and fold under there because it was so thin.

It was fast, so terribly fast, as it shrugged the bed aside and came after her. Iris was appalled by how swift its ungainly limbs were as it clawed towards her. Her stomach wrenched with a horror so complete that her legs almost gave way. She threw herself downstairs, three at a time and then, before she reached the bottom, she jumped over the banister, landing on all fours and sprinting back down the hall in the opposite direction, towards the kitchen.

The crooked faery raced to the bottom of the stairs, its greater speed and weight giving it a momentum that propelled him beyond the foot of the stairs and it slid towards the front door. Then its huge claws dug into the floorboards and it was after her. She saw its fanged grin as she whipped into the kitchen, and she sobbed with relief to see that a lantern was still lit on the sideboard.

She skinned her knees as she slid across the floor and threw back the trapdoor. *A place to keep a few things* her father had called it, but it was mostly filled with things he had wanted out of sight. She had to force aside unseen objects, bottles fell and rolled as she dived in and scrambled under the floorboards. It was a shallow space. With her elbow against the old flagstones, her fingertips brushed the floor-boards above. It was just big enough for a child. Hopefully not big enough for the monster behind her. Iris could barely even crawl. She had to drag herself, pushing with her feet to get as far away as she could from the trap door, clambering over leftover floorboards and shoving aside wooden boxes.

The crooked faery creaked along the floorboards above her. Its head leaned into the hole, and its face was so horrible she almost looked away. Gleaming eyes and corpse-coloured skin, and powerful jaws filled with filthy fangs. It grinned and reached for her, swiping an arm longer than her leg, its fingers tipped with claws like knives. It grabbed for her again, and she screamed as the tip of its jagged nails lashed her ankle. She banged her head in panic as she tried to move in the restricted space and shuffled, sobbing, out of its reach.

She screamed her sister's name once, loud and piercing. Her voice was deafening in the tiny space, and Iris clamped her fingers over her mouth, forcing herself to be silent. Katie wasn't home, Iris was almost sure of it. Even if her sister was in the house, she wouldn't be able to save Iris anyway. All that would happen if Katie tried to help, Iris realised, is that Iris would have to listen to Katie die.

Iris's breathing was fast and erratic as she tried to battle hysteria. Past her trembling hands she looked back at the trap door. The crooked faery leaned in and looked around, its head twitching fast from side to side. For a moment as it forced its narrow shoulders into the space, Iris thought it would be able to fold and fit under the floorboards in the same way that it had hidden under her bed. Its crooked spine flexed like a stretching cat, but then its elbows banged against the wood, and it snarled and retreated.

The space under the kitchen floor was dark and dusty. The lantern light showed in thin lines of gold through the little gaps in the floorboards above. Iris could see almost nothing of the kitchen.

Wood creaked above her as the crooked faery moved, its distorted shadow blocking the light as it leaned over her. Through the crack in the floorboards, she saw its eyes. They were pale grey, with snake-like pupils which flared and reflected the lantern-light. Its teeth chattered and it ground its jaws. Warm saliva dripped onto her cheek, and she screamed with disgust. '*Leave me alone!*'

The slit pupils narrowed. It rasped laughter as it leaned back.

Its huge claws smashed into the wood above her face, sending splinters flying. With the second blow its claws cut deeper. Iris scuttled sideways and it followed, hammering at the floor with its hands. One of its blows hit a weak point in the wood, and a floorboard cracked at its centre. Iris put her hand over her mouth to stop herself from screaming again and tried to move as quietly as she could. She wriggled, using her elbows and heels to push her forward. Claws slammed through the floorboards again, inches from her stomach. She rolled away and the sharp dirty edges of its talons caught on her clothing.

On her stomach she shuffled under the shadow of the kitchen table. The crooked faery threw it over, but when it crashed upside down, Iris crawled beneath it again. The table was good, heavy wood, and it offered some protection. The monster could shove it aside, but the table slowed its attacks every time she crawled back beneath the temporary shield.

It roared in frustration and paused its attacks, dragging its claws over the floorboards, the sound of its talon-tips scraping over the wood made her shudder. It ground its teeth again and saliva spattered on the wood. Then it laughed again. It moved to the centre of the kitchen and began pounding at the floorboards as though she were lying there. For a moment, as it began punching and clawing furiously, Iris thought it had lost track of where she was. As she fought to catch her breath she realised, if the crooked faery made a big enough hole in the centre of the room, it would be easier for it to reach her with its long arms, wherever she crawled. She put her hands over her face as planks started to splinter. It would probably tear up the whole floor to get to her. Iris rubbed away tears, rolled over slowly, and began to move as quietly as she could towards the hall.

Above her, partition walls separated the kitchen, the hall and the dining room. Here, against the flagstones of the old house, there was no dividing wall. Iris crept quietly beneath the hall floor, searching for a spot under the staircase. She probed with her fingertips, searching for a break in the even lines of the floorboards… and there! The cupboard under the stairs did not have finished flooring. The planks in there were the rough, unvarnished leftovers, and had not been nailed down. The cupboard floor was one of the many things that her father did not consider to be *at the top of his list*.

Iris raised her feet and carefully lifted out and then lowered a wide piece of planking. She set it down next to her, wincing in case it clattered. The crooked faery was making as much noise as a crew of workmen, but she was terrified it would hear her. She removed a second board, cringed as an old boot fell through the gap. Then she shuffled sideways and sat up in the darkness of the cupboard. She hesitated. It might be safer to hide in the cupboard, try to barricade the door with loose floorboards and hope that, when the faery leaned down to look for her, it thought she had escaped.

She carefully considered what to do next. Then she climbed up fully into the cupboard under the stairs, her teeth gritted with fear of knocking things over and giving herself away. She opened the door and looked up the dark hallway. She wanted to run back up the stairs to her room, lock everything, and hide in her heavy oak wardrobe. But the stairs creaked. If the crooked faery heard her or caught a glimpse of her through the kitchen door, she would never be able to outrun it. Iris bit her lip and slipped into the dining room. The table was still covered in the dinner dishes. The maid would come in the morning and...

Iris shook her head. What would the maid find if she came in the morning? What would the maid think when she saw the kitchen ripped apart like mad axemen had been trapped inside? Would the maid find her family grieving? If the crooked faery stayed in the house, would the maid find anybody left alive at all? Iris crept across the room and grabbed a knife from the table. It looked pitifully small, but she meant it for a tool, not a weapon.

She unlocked and opened a window slowly and quietly, then sat and swung her legs over the sill to stand, uncertainly, in the night. She never went outside at night. Her instincts told her to run. To run and scream and hope she somehow made it up the long lane before the monster caught her, but she knew it was far too fast. It would be foolish to run, and there was nobody to hear her scream.

Iris moved quickly along the side of the house and entered the orchard. She could still hear the crashing and hacking of the crooked faery when she reached the tree that grew beside her window and climbed it for the very first time. It was easy, even in the darkness. Once she had hauled herself up into the low branches, the light from her bedroom window provided enough illumination to find handholds and make her way carefully along the narrowing branch nearest to the house. She could see pale scars in the bark where the crooked faery's claws had cut into the branches when it had climbed inside.

With the butter knife it was easy to lift the loose latch and then swing the window open. She could imagine the faery using just a single claw to do the same. As Iris pried the window open, everything fell silent in the house.

The darkness of the orchard yawned beneath her, and Iris was gripped with such fear that she struggled to put one leg on the sill and climb inside. The window was not quite wide enough or high enough for her to duck under the frame. She threw the blunt knife onto the floor and with sweating hands, panic making her clumsy, Iris gave up on trying to climb carefully and instead dived through headfirst. She slid awkwardly half upside-down, palms flat on the floor, then rolled forward and sat up, breathless. She got up, but before she could move to close the door, she caught sight of the crooked faery's eyes, shining with reflected lantern light as it came up the stairs. Iris cried out and, as it clawed onto the landing, she grabbed the lantern and threw it as hard as she could.

The faery slashed at the lantern defensively, shearing through the glass reservoir. As the lantern shattered, oil showered everywhere. The flame bloomed and ignited with a roar. The crooked faery jumped back, clawing where its forearm was covered with oil and on fire. Reflected flames flickered in its eyes as it opened its mouth and roared with fury. It charged through the fire that was spreading across the landing floor, but Iris had only needed a moment to reach her door and swung it shut with a crash. The faery clawed the other side and it rattled in its frame. Her shaking fingers found the key in the lock and turned it. Then she pulled at her wardrobe, her strength fuelled by panic, hauling on it until it tipped. As the heavy wooden wardrobe fell against the door, Iris jumped aside, but one of the doors fell open, cracking against her head. She fell, half-stunned. Terrified of fainting she forced herself up to her knees and crawled slowly to the window. She first pulled the shutters closed and latched them, and then latched the window as securely as she could. Now the crooked faery could not easily come in that way. The bedroom door was still leaping and rattled in its frame as the monster thrashed itself against the door in fury. The wardrobe had effectively barricaded it shut. The banging ceased and the *croque-mitaine* let out a raw scream of fury.

Iris heard the whispering crackle of flames and was only grateful that the fire was now burning high enough to drive the crooked faery back from her door. Her head hurt and she tried to feel her way to the bed in the dark, but dizziness and nausea made her sit down on the floor and lean her head against the covers instead. She could not help sliding sideways to lay down and she closed her eyes, knowing there was nothing else that she could do to protect herself.

She jerked awake to the stink of smoke, in suffocating darkness. There was the sound of men's voices shouting outside. Iris realised that, at last, people had come to help. The fire had spread. She could hear its crackling beyond her bedroom door but was more grateful than scared. People had come to help because of the fire. She wasn't alone anymore.

She struggled to sit up and crawled, feeling nauseous, to the window. She fumbled to get it open, unlatched the shutters with slow fingers, and heard the voices of two men calling up to her window urgently. The night was lit with flames and the stars were blotted out by smoke.

Iris's bones felt like water, and she could hardly stay standing, let alone climb down. She had barely begun to try when one of the young men scrambled into the tree and grabbed her under the arms, pulling her free from the window, and swinging her down to his friend. She knew they were asking her questions, but their words did not make sense.

'My head hurts,' she said. Where she touched her scalp, her fingers came away wet.

As they set her down, she could not help staring behind them into the darkness, wondering where the crooked faery was. Her legs gave way and she fell hard. The orchard grass was cool against her palms and the side of her face. The man who had pulled her from the window lifted her up and carried her like a little child. The men hurried with her around to the front of the house, where a crowd was forming, and set her down. Some people were running back and forth from the well with buckets of water, but the blaze was fierce. The flames had not yet reached the stables, but the horses had been led out. The animals seemed unconcerned as they stood by the lane flicking their tails.

Someone laid a wet cloth on Iris's forehead. She felt a chipped cup pressed into her hands and she gulped down water until it was empty. A lady was asking her a question, gently, but insistently. Iris finally understood her when she asked, in accented English, 'Who was in the house?'

Iris looked at the dark woods before she said, 'It was the crooked faery. *La crocque-mitaine.* But I think it's gone now.'

'I'm sorry? I don't understand you. I mean who else, other than you, was in the house before the fire started?'

'Just the *crocque-mitaine,* Madame.'

The lady tilted her head, and Iris could see she didn't understand. Then more people were running down the lane and Iris heard her mother screaming. Drunk and screaming and then kneeling on the floor with her hands in her hair staring at the burning house. Iris saw her father stumble to a halt, his mouth hanging open.

'Is this your house? Is this your daughter?' The lady called to them, 'Your little girl is bleeding. I think she's in shock. There's soot under her nose. She probably breathed some smoke, but she's safe.'

Her mother struggled up, reaching for her. Iris moved towards her, arms out for a hug, then stumbled when her mother began shaking her. Fingers digging into Iris's arms, breath and voice sharp with whisky, her mother screamed, 'What have you done? Iris, you stupid girl, *what have you done?* What did I tell you about lighting candles?'

Her father pulled her aside and shouted a different question.

'Where's Katie? Iris, where is your sister?'

'I don't know.'

'Iris, *where's Katie?*'

'I don't know!' Iris screamed.

Her father strode away and stared through the broken frame of the front door. It was splintered where somebody had kicked it down. Inside, the staircase looked like a waterfall of flame flowing upwards.

'Anyone in there will be trapped… and the smoke…' a man holding a bucket shrugged helplessly.

'No,' said Iris. 'Katie gets out over the stable roof. Out her window. She does it all the time.'

'Then where is she?' Her father was turning hopelessly, looking for his other daughter.

'I don't know!' Iris started to cry. 'I don't *know*! I screamed. If she was here, she would have run! She must have run! Mum, was she even here when you left?'

She could see by her parents faces that they didn't know.

Fear coiled like a cold snake in Iris's stomach, and she had to be sure that Katie wasn't in her room. Her father shouted as Iris broke into a run. He followed as she scrambled up the woodpile and struggled to follow as she ran unsteadily along the apex of the stable roof. He called to her again as she edged out onto the gable towards her sister's window, but she ignored him.

The window was open, smoke pouring into the sky. The air was too hot to breathe, and it was like leaning into an oven, but Iris pushed her head inside to make sure Katie wasn't there. Inside, the doorway was framed in flames and Iris could clearly see that the room was empty. For a second, she felt relief. Then she realised that the doorframe was broken. The lock shattered, the door off its hinges.

Blood was smeared across the floor beside the bed and splattered on the white linen. A red handprint. Drag-marks through streaks of blood.

Arms wrapped around Iris. She fought her father as he tried to pick her up. Fought the same way that her sister would have fought when the crooked faery took her. Blood and flame blurred together as tears distorted Iris's vision.

'Why did you leave us?' she screamed. 'Why would you leave us?' And she couldn't stop fighting, as he lifted her and carried her down.

CHANGELINGS

Black and chill are Their nights on the wold
And They live so long and They feel no pain:
I shall grow up, but never grow old,
I shall always, always be very cold,
I shall never come back again!

Charlotte Mew

Carrie Harker leant her back up against the white stone and closed her eyes. Tears spilled between her lashes, and she did not bother to wipe them away. She held her baby son and tried not to listen to the weak rasp of his breathing. She somehow expected every weak exhalation to be the last, but he struggled a new pained inhalation each time. Every day weaker. Every night his breathing more strained.

He no longer cried.

Amory, she had named him, for his father who had been lost at sea while she was pregnant. Amory for the man she had loved. Who had given her a son with the same red hair, who might have grown to have the same laughing eyes and easy smile. She had hoped her son would give her something of the man she had lost. In the first hours after his birth, she had understood that would never be the case.

The whisper of the midwife had carried from the next room.

'Something's wrong.'

'Please,' she had begged, 'Tell me what's happening.'

The doctor's expression had told her all she really needed to know before he said, 'There's nothing I can do.'

The doctor no longer met her eyes. Nor would the priest who spoke of a God that gathered the sweetest souls soonest. The local women came less and less, except to look and to wait, and to carry news of the Irish widow with the dying child back to town. To gossip and speculate whether she had ever *really* been married.

'Please, Amory,' she whispered and didn't even know whether she was begging the dead father or the dying son. 'I need you. Please don't leave me alone.'

Carrie was exhausted, but too scared to sleep. She only listened and waited as the hours ground away in grey solitude, until the sound of his ragged breaths in the silent house had been too much to bear.

As evening closed to darkness Carrie decided she had to get out. She walked towards the woods, where the birds were gathering to sleep, and singing their twilight chorus. She wandered down a rabbit path, between two fields and sat down against a tall, pale stone.

In a half-delirium of exhaustion she rested, dozed, and then blinked tear-reddened eyes at the warm glow of sunlight. She thought, momentarily afraid, that she had fallen asleep and woken to the glare of dawn. But above her the sky was dark, and the light only radiated from a woman in an exquisite white dress, with long golden hair.

The landscape had changed. Only the stone remained the same. Around her trees twisted and the night was lit with fireflies and soft glowing toadstools. Everywhere rabbits ran and glowing flowers bloomed. The fields were gone and wild, wild woods stretched as far as she could see.

The woman knelt beside Mrs Harker, who watched her without any particular fear. Absolute despair is its own protection and Carrie Harker had nothing much left to lose.

'You're one of the fair folk, my Lady?' Carrie asked.

She knew the legends. She'd been raised with them.

The woman nodded and then leaned to look at the baby.

'Can you help him, my Lady?' Carrie asked. 'Forgive my impertinence in asking for faery favours, but he is suffering so.'

Her tears came again. This time she dashed them away impatiently to say urgently, 'I'll offer you anything for your help. He's all I have left, my little Amory. My husband is dead, and I know that sometimes deals can be made with the fair folk. I would gladly give you *anything* you want. My soul, or my service for a hundred years. For a *thousand* years, if you wish. If there's anything I have, anything I can give, if you can just make him well...'

But the lady was shaking her head regretfully.

'What you wish for is not within my power,' she said. 'My gifts are of a different nature.'

The lady met her eyes and Carrie found that they were kind and dark and wise. The woman in white was the first person who had held her gaze since Amory had been born.

'Can you help him at all?' Carrie asked. 'Can you ease his pain? Please, if there's anything you can do...'

The woman in white nodded sadly, 'I can take his pain away until it is over.' Then for a moment her gaze flashed away and a thoughtful line creased between her brows.

'Please,' Carrie whispered, 'I would give anything to ease his pain. What I offered to you before, I offer again. In truth, I don't wish to be alone, so if I may be of service...'

'I ask nothing in return for this small kindness,' the lady said slowly. 'I only ask that you consider kindness in turn, when it is needed. There are always those who need help, after all.'

When her eyes met Carrie's again there was a considering look in them. Carrie was vaguely aware that white roses were growing around them while they sat, budding, blooming in soft white blossoms.

'You cannot save him then?' Carrie nodded acceptance. 'If you can spare him some pain, then I am grateful. It is an honour to meet one of the folk, even in a time of such grief.'

The lady in white placed her fingers on Amory's brow and whispered, 'Peace now, little one. Time to sleep.'

She stood, and helped Carrie to her feet.

'Return home now,' she said. 'Go home and rest. Remember that your grief need not be complete.'

She touched a finger to Carrie's brow, then placed a palm to the white stone and was gone.

The loss of the lady's light made her feel blind and Carrie blinked and breathed for a few long moments until she could see in the dusk again. She was back near the narrow path between fields where she had first sat down. She felt oddly peaceful and supposed it was the gift of a faery touch.

Amory slept in her arms.

She'd heard the fae spoke in riddles, and she was not sure she understood, or was meant to understand, all that had been said. She was certain now that not God, nor man, nor even magic could help her son.

There was nothing left to do.

She walked home and lay Amory gently in his crib and kissed his forehead. Then she went to lay upon her own bed. She fell into peaceful delirium. She dreamt of light and white roses, and a voice speaking gently to a child.

She woke in the morning and, as awareness returned, she listened for the sound of her baby's laboured breathing. She heard nothing. Fear ran cold fingers over her until she gripped her blankets, too afraid to turn, too afraid to look, straining to hear anything.

Silence from the crib.

Birdsong and the smell of roses outside.

Carrie forced herself to swing her feet to the floorboards. The fear was like a weight on her chest. Each movement was a separate struggle, to pull back her blankets, to push herself to her feet, and then to put one foot in front of the other.

Amory lay in the crib. He was still. Paler than he had ever been, and his fine red hair seemed even more vivid against his white skin.

She reached out a hand to touch his cheek, expecting his skin to be cold. Expecting the brief suffering of his life to be over.

The baby's skin was cool but, at the touch of her hand, he turned his head and opened his eyes.

His eyes were as black as pitch.

Carrie's scream was raw and brief as she recoiled with her hands over her mouth, falling against her bed, then running from the room and slamming the door. She ran into the garden, into the light of day. It was cool, and clear, and everywhere white roses were blooming where there hadn't been roses before. They wound and twisted along her fence, in delicate patterns, as though trained by a master gardener for decades. Cascades of white blooms that all seemed to originate from a single point.

She followed the slender, green lateral stems back around the house to where the branches were thicker and darker, to two twining trunks with low branches that twisted in embrace before throwing out thorny arms in all directions. Carrie imagined them growing and coiling around the garden's edge as she slept. While her dying son was lifted in fair hands, and then replaced with something else.

She sat down where the roses grew to form a bower, near the tangle of roots where white petals fell like snow. A single white rose had been plucked and laid upon the earth.

This was her son's grave then.

She rested her head and soaked the ground with tears of grief and fear. With terror that she might be going mad, and with rage at the brutal cruelty of life. Then slowly, with great heaving sobs, she wept with release, because her son was free from pain.

It was some time before she could bring herself to re-enter the house. Her breathing came in swift, panting gasps as she walked to the bedroom. Slowly she shuffled her bare feet forward until she could see it. The thing in the crib that looked like her son. Her heart hammered as it looked at her. A black unblinking gaze.

'What are you?' Carrie asked, 'Can you understand me? I know you're not my son. God help me… am I going mad? If you can talk, then please talk.'

The red lashes of the child fluttered and finally he blinked. It was the uncertain gaze of wild things ready to bolt. Carrie found herself thinking of a fawn she had almost stumbled over as a child. A beautiful thing all dappled and afraid as it watched her. It had been so still and silent, laying unmoving, hoping its camouflage would be enough to save it from a predator's jaws. The same gentle words she'd spoken then slipped from her now.

'I'm not going to hurt you…'

She made herself lean closer, staring at this thing so like her son, ready to jerk her head back if it moved.

There were perhaps a few differences only a mother would notice. His hair was redder, his facial features a little sharper. Nothing a stranger would notice. He was so very alike, and babies all looked much the same, after all. This baby looked so much like her son that she wanted to reach for him. It was like finding a strange, unexpected twin.

Except for those eyes.

The way his head rested to one side was not the helpless loll of a baby, but the curious tilt of an animal regarding something new. The faery who had brought him here had seemed seelie and fair. Surely she would not have brought something evil and unseelie into Carrie's home.

'What on earth am I supposed to do with you?' Carrie whispered, then took a deep breath and swallowed. 'Right then. Let's have a look at you, I suppose. If you bite me, little one, I swear on all that's good and pure in the world that I will throw you directly into the sea…'

The baby tilted its head the other way as she reached for it, a swift, wary movement and raised a hand. A hand with fingers just slightly too long for a baby, held up in a weak defence.

A faery child wearing her dead son's image like a mask. All that was left of her son now was faery glamour.

Would this faery boy grow and change as her son would have? Would she see how her child would have looked as he took his first steps? Would it be her son's voice when this creature spoke his first words? Would this little creature grow to look like the boy, and then the man, her son might have become? Would he learn from her in the same way?

Or would he be terribly, horribly, *different*?

Carrie shivered but extended her hand. As they touched, his little fingers gripped uncertainly around her thumb. Stronger than a new-born should be, but still frail. Warily Carrie drew back the blanket. He was thin, but not malnourished. There was a steady rise and fall in his chest, a pattern of breathing that suggested the child was nervous, but his lungs were clear. He breathed easily. He breathed well.

'No hooves at least,' Carrie said to him.

Her true son had a small birthmark on his shoulder, and she slid her hand under the new infant carefully to see if it was there.

'I'm going to turn you,' she said, and rolled him gently so she could better see his back.

She released him and her hands flew to her mouth at the sight of the wound. Three slash marks, so deep they would surely have killed a human baby with the force of the blow alone.

But this was not a human baby.

The wounds were pink and healthy, and they looked to be healing very swiftly. Nothing so extreme should heal so fast. The little creature wriggled a bit in discomfort as she checked the wounds more closely for any sign of infection. She soothed him automatically with a hush and the stroke of her hand. He grasped at her again and she let him hold onto her thumb as she rolled him back.

'What *happened* to you? You poor little thing! How did you survive this?'

What had the lady in white said?

There are always those that need help.

'Well. If you're as alone as I am, I suppose it wouldn't hurt for you to stay for a little while. Just until you're better. Or however long you need, I suppose. What do you think about that?'

A knock at the front door made her jump half out of her skin. Her hand flew to her heart. The wild black eyes of the infant flashed with fear, his gaze fixed on her, little hands clasping the edge of his blanket with reflexive panic.

'Mrs Harker?' A male voice called.

She heard the door open and then a woman's voice called out, 'Carrie?'

'Oh, sweet heavens defend us,' Carrie winced and whispered. 'Father Scott and Emma Le Brocq, the local gossip.'

They walked in before Carrie could think of a way to stop them. She placed her body between the doorway and the cradle. She saw Mrs Le Brocq notice her bare muddy feet. Saw the woman's eyes flick around the mess of the room and the unmade bed.

'Oh Carrie! You look stricken! Is he gone then, poor little soul?'

'No!' Carrie said. 'No, he's so much better, thank you, but he's sleeping so if you wouldn't mind…'

Before Carrie could begin to usher them from the room, Father Scott had taken a firm hold of her hand and begun to compliment her on her roses, and Emma Le Brocq had squeezed past her.

'You better let me check, my dear,' Mrs Le Brocq said and leaned over the cradle.

Carrie winced as Emma let out a scream.

'Oh lord! Oh saints preserve us!' the village woman cried. 'Look at his eyes, Father! Look at his eyes!'

The priest moved past Carrie and then recoiled, colour draining from his cheeks.

Carrie felt panic grip her.

'Good Lord, what has happened to him?' Father Scott shouted.

'He's *fine*,' Carrie tried to say, but Emma Le Brocq's hysterics drowned her words.

'It's not her baby, Father!' The Village woman cried. 'It's faery work and a faery child. A *P'tit Faitot*! Oh, what can we do to get rid of it?'

'You'll do *nothing* to him!' Carrie said in horror.

'I heard tell of a husband and wife in Guernsey, whose child was replaced with a changeling just like this one,' the woman said. 'The couple were cooking limpets in the embers of the hearth and the baby stood straight in its cot as the limpets bubbled and swore aloud, *"I'm not of this year, not the year before, nor yet of the time of King John of yore, but in all my days, and years, I ween, so many pots boiling I never have seen."* Fortunately…'

Mrs Le Brocq stepped forward to eye the cradle. '*Fortunately* that mother knew the ways of the faeries and all of the old stories. She knew that she needed to throw this changeling creature onto the fire.

That way, you see, the faery mother that had stolen the human baby would come back for own child and give back the human child.'

'Throw a *baby* onto a fire...?' Carrie said faintly.

'It is strange,' said Father Scott ponderously, edging away. 'That if a mother faery cared so much about her child, that she would leave it behind in the first place.'

Mrs Le Brocq nodded. 'In that particular case, as soon as the human mother lifted that changeling to throw it on the fire, the faery mother jumped through the window! It replaced the *real* baby boy in the cot and stole the changeling away again. We should build a fire. Or wait, what else harms faeries? Let me think...'

A breeze drifted through the window, carrying with it the scent of roses.

'If you touch my baby,' Carrie said firmly. 'I will kill you.'

Father Scott looked discomforted, glancing from Carrie to Emma Le Brocq, to the black eyes of the baby. His fingers fumbled with his rosary.

'Your son was sick,' Emma Le Brocq spoke to Carrie as though she was a fool. 'The sort of sick that *doesn't get better*, my dear. He was born wrong. He didn't cry. He didn't feed. Don't you see, Carrie? This *thing* is not your baby!'

'Don't talk about him that way! His name,' snapped Carrie, pointing at the cot, 'is *Amory*. And he is my *son*. You think I don't know my own son?'

'Its eyes are black, Carrie. Look at it!' Emma whispered. 'It's a *monster*. How can you not see it?'

'Babies' eyes change colour,' Carrie said with forced calm. 'Everybody knows that. Besides,' Carrie began to lie, shrugging and raising her chin defiantly, 'my husband had an uncle with eyes black as coal. A family trait it is. My little Amory's eyes have been changing colour since he was born. Every day darker and darker blue. And now here we are and they're black as obsidian.'

Carrie let no uncertainty or fear show through as she shook her head and forced a wild, false laugh. 'You come in here, Mrs Le Brocq, with your *superstitions*. You realise you sound quite mad, don't you? And you, Father!' She turned on the priest. 'I'm surprised at you listening to this talk of faeries and whatnot. *Changelings* if you please! Throwing babies on fires! What kind of ungodly talk is that? What would your parishioners think if they knew?'

She turned back to Emma Le Brocq and folded her arms. 'I suppose you think he'll be crawling up the walls and eating the neighbourhood cats next, do you?' She let very real tears begin to fill her eyes and drip onto her cheeks. 'You came expecting my son to be *dead* and now there's not enough *drama* for you to take back to your knitting circle, is that it, Emma? Well he's *not* dead. He's getting better.'

Emma Le Brocq eyed her with a twisted expression of pity and disbelief, saying. 'Carrie, do try to be reasonable. You need our help. That *isn't* your son, and I can prove it. They say faeries don't like iron. Perhaps if we just put the poker against his skin and see what happens.'

'Poke my son with a poker?' Carrie clenched her fists and let all the fear and anger she had felt since she had given birth show in her voice. 'If you so much as *glance* towards that fireplace, I will take that poker and beat you senseless with it, you horse-faced bully of a woman!'

Hysteria had been clawing up inside her for days and letting it out now was almost a relief. Carrie drew herself up to her full height and with every scrap of rage and grief she had been holding in since her son was born, she screamed. 'Get out of my house, you pair of useless idiots! Get out with your damn superstitions and false sympathy. First you act like my son is dying. Now he has a bit of colour in his cheeks, you tell me he's a *changeling*? You're enough to drive a woman mad! Get out both of you, don't you ever darken my door again! And I swear on my life that if you ever try to touch my baby, you will regret it until your dying days – and your dying days won't be far off if you even look sideways at my Amory again. Now get out! Out, out, *out!*'

She chased them to the front door and slammed it behind them.

Exhausted and utterly deflated Carrie returned to the bedroom and sank down next to the crib. She rested her head on the carved wooden dowels. She was trembling and had to take a few long breaths before she could open her eyes.

The baby had rolled as best he could onto his side and was regarding her with what looked very like concern. He reached out his hand again and she smiled.

'Not much of a cryer are you, little lad?'

She looked into his black eyes and for the first time she found them strangely beautiful.

'This won't be easy,' she said. 'I'll need to grieve my boy and put on an act. We won't have anybody but each other. But I won't turn away a child in need, and you are truly a *child*, I can see that much.'

She stood up and carefully lifted him into her arms. He seemed uncertain, blinking up at her as she held him, relaxing when she gave him her finger to hold.

'Perhaps a faery boy will be a blessing when all's said and done,' Carrie said softly. 'The fair folk must have given you to me for a reason, and their reasons are their own, no doubt, but you're my son now, and I'll always treat you so. So you just behave yourself. Don't go eating any cats, or climbing the walls, or reciting verse about limpets, do you hear? And there'll be no disappearing back to the land of the fae without telling me when you'll be home for dinner. Lord, listen to me, will you?' she sighed. 'I sound as mad as a bucket.'

Carrie walked to the window and looked out at her garden of white roses.

'It's not your name... it's *his* name. But you'd better get used to being called Amory Harker. And if you have another name? Well, maybe one day, when you're old enough to find out what it is... Maybe you'll tell me, son.'

REVENANTS

From the body of one guilty deed a thousand ghostly fears and haunting thoughts proceed.

William Wordsworth

'So they're having a midnight wedding *after* a wake.'

'Yes! I know it's not traditional, Paul, but it's what Mary and Gabbon want. It's strange, but not as strange as the fact that those two haven't killed each other before they made it to their wedding day.'

Paul laughed. 'Do you think our encounter with an evil black dog gave those two a taste for the macabre?'

Nelia took his hand as they walked down the hill towards a dark and silent sea. 'Possibly,' she admitted. 'They're certainly enjoying telling the tale of that night over and over again. Mary won't replace the tavern door because she says it attracts more customers when people come to see the hole with the scratch marks and the burns. *Oh*! Did I tell you that Gabbon's been talking about getting a black puppy and calling it Tchico?'

'Ha! I hope he does. Stop fussing with your hair. You look beautiful. Are you sure the party is *here*, Nelia? Isn't the church on the other side of the bay?'

'It's definitely here! Trust me. Mary gave me *very* detailed instructions about this evening – you wouldn't believe me if I told you. All you need to know is we're having the wake here, then walking through the faery woods to get to St Brelade's church just before midnight. Oh, look at all the flowers and ribbons on the inn! Haven't they done it out nice?'

Paul stopped to look at the beautiful granite building, and wrinkled his nose when he read the hand-painted sign above the tavern door. 'Is this place truly called The Old Smugglers Inn? That's practically *taunting* the excise men, isn't it?'

'Yes, apparently all the constabulary drink here. This was where smugglers and pirates drank for centuries before it was even a real tavern, so it's well named. Come on, Paul! I'm sure Mary will explain everything to you at some point.'

She grabbed his hand to pull him inside. As the heavy oak door opened, sounds of laughter and loud conversation spilled out into the night. They pushed through a tight crowd of men at the foot of some stairs to find the wedding party. Mary was not hard to spot, as she had been given a raised chair on a crate, all decorated in white flowers, like a throne in an enclosed area of the inn. She beckoned them with an imperious hand and stood to greet Nelia with a kiss on each cheek.

Paul was captured in a firm handshake by Gabbon, who said, 'Weird-shaped pub, isn't it? Used to be two fisherman's cottages next to each other.'

'Why are you two having your wedding in Jersey, when you both live in Guernsey?' Paul captured the cantankerous woman in a fond hug. 'And why in *this* inn, when you own your own tavern, Mary?'

Mary gave a dry laugh and reached for her glass, 'Do you really think I want everybody drinking my own bar dry? And having an excuse *not* to pay because it's a party? No thank you very much!'

'Mary's a barmaid, so most of the people she knows are alcoholics,' added Gabbon with a wink, 'we realised we'd save a fortune just by getting on a boat.'

'And we have another reason as well,' Mary exchanged a glance with Gabbon, then she clasped her hands together. 'Right that's the last of the people I care about, so we may as well get on with this.'

Gabbon gave her a serious nod. Mary stood on her chair, clapped her hands, and shouted for silence with the sort of volume only a life-long barmaid could manage.

'I still don't really understand why we're in Jersey, and not in Guernsey,' Paul complained in a whisper.

'Listen,' Nelia said, 'and you'll find out.'

Of the five people who had been besieged by the tower dog, only Kemp was not to be seen. Paul glanced around for his telltale cloud of pipe smoke but couldn't spot him. Pockets of conversation continued in the other two rooms of the tavern until Gabbon roared, 'Shut up when a lady's talking!'

The bar rooms fell into shocked silence, and people pushed closer to see what was happening, adding to the crush. Mary nodded and began to speak.

'When I heard that my favourite aunt in Jersey had died so unexpectedly, and so close to when my wedding was planned, I knew I wanted to honour her. So here we are. A wake before a wedding.'

Mary threw her arms wide, and Paul noticed that the white flowers decorating the beams were tied with black ribbons.

'I knew Aunt Catherine when I was just a little girl, and what I remember best about her was how much she *loved* ghost stories. I know her son will agree, won't you Christian?' She pointed towards a confused-looking young man sat alone at the bar. When everyone turned to look at him he displayed all the discomfort of youth, hunching slightly and flattening his lips in a tight approximation of a smile as he nodded uncertainly.

'I've told him how important it is to me that he be here tonight,' Mary went on. 'Catherine was my favourite family member. We didn't see each other much after she moved to Jersey. Never even got to tell her how I was nearly eaten by a giant dog from the very coldest hell! She'd have loved that.' Mary wiped away a fake tear.

'She'd have appreciated the path we've chosen tonight. A walk through faery woods from a haunted inn and then through a church graveyard where everybody knows monsters lurk.' There was some muttering at this, and Mary continued. 'Yes, I know! We've all heard of the Faery Woods. You are protected if you keep to the path... ah, but even then you may not be safe. The ancient things that lurk *there* can sniff out evil in the hearts of men. They say those woods on the hill are guarded by *Lé Tchéziot*, the one they call the Devil's deputy. A hooded monster of such ancient evil and power that nobody can refuse its call – not men, nor women, nor even other monsters. If that thing whispers to you from the night, you *will* step from the path, whether you want to or not.'

'It feasts on dark souls,' a nervous voice said from the back of the crowd.

'They say the White Lady protects those who wander where they shouldn't,' said a large lady in a large bonnet.

'Yes,' Mary agreed. 'But *La Blianche Femme* does not protect evil men. Evil men belong to the darkness…'

'But it is a *beautiful* walk in the moonlight, and we just won't stray from the path,' Gabbon said dispassionately. 'It'll be a lovely stroll.'

'Then round the bay to the graveyard,' Mary continued. 'Oh, how Catherine would have loved that! The legend of the Ghouls! Tell it Gabbon! This is your island, I'll not speak ill of the place,' Mary said folding her arms.

Gabbon snorted at this statement, since Mary spoke ill of Jersey at every opportunity. *Especially* if her fiancé was there to hear it. Then he remembered himself and assumed a dramatic pose. He spread his fingers like claws and raised his voice to a booming pitch.

'We all know that this area is famous for evil men! Since the thirteenth century this place was a haven for pirates and smugglers. The worst of men and the darkest of deeds. Thieves and murderers who came and went in the night. They were dark and dreadful days, and some of the men who died were so evil that they could not stay dead. Their compatriots tried burying them in the graveyard of St Brelade's Church, but it didn't take.' He shook his head solemnly. 'Those hallowed grounds would not suffer their evil to seep into it. It changed them and spat them out. Not as ghosts, you see, but as flesh and blood monsters that spend their wretched nights feasting on the flesh of other evil men. Vile deeds never wash off the hands of those who commit them, they linger and stink, and ghouls know the smell of evil-tainted meat. They dig down into the graves and feast. Mindless, vicious beasts, gorging on corpses.'

'And if they cannot find enough dead flesh,' Mary put in. 'If an evil man or woman crosses their path…'

'Oh it's best never to cross a graveyard at night,' Gabbon shook his head dramatically. 'Not if you are cruel or wicked. Ghouls are waiting. Starving. Hungering beneath the earth for those with the scent of the sepulchre on their skin.'

Paul and Nelia exchanged glances as Gabbon gave them a nearly imperceptible wink.

'Whistling!' Somebody shouted from the back of the room. 'If you whistle as you walk through the graveyard, the ghouls won't get you. Otherwise, they might reach up and grab your foot.'

'They don't like fire,' somebody else piped up. 'Fire and light and whistling.'

'Why whistling?' asked Paul, but Nelia elbowed him gently and shook her head.

'Not now,' she whispered. 'They're not done.'

Mary clapped for attention and began to speak again. 'Before the wedding, though, we'll finish the wake! In honour of my favourite aunt, who loved them, I will tell you a ghost story! You'll like this one, Christian!'

Mary's young cousin did not look like he was enjoying anything. His fingers turned an empty glass on the bar. Gabbon shouted, 'Adrian if you will be so good as to darken the lanterns, and snuff a few candles...?'

The barman nodded, set down a glass and cloth, and moved to blow out lanterns and lower the light in the rooms. Shadows grew and faces became indistinct. Smoke from snuffed candles drifted to the ceiling and hung, a heavy blue, in the soft light.

Mary spoke again, more softly, so that people leaned in to hear. Chairs creaked as bodies shifted, a few men from the far room quickly moved to stand by the door where they could hear better as she began.

'The Old Smuggler's Inn is haunted!' Mary glanced around, feigning fear. Men and women in their wedding finery turned as though expecting a phantom to walk through the wall, as she said, 'Many years ago, this place was filled with wicked men. One night, the innkeeper's wife walked out back to fetch some wood... and stumbled upon an act of murder! A pirate was brutally stabbing a man that he had lured outside. For gold? For vengeance? Over a petty insult or just in a drunken rage? Who can say? Evil men *always* swear there was a good reason. The innkeeper's wife was terrified, and she turned to run, but the pirate was faster. He knew he would be hanged if she told the authorities what he had done. He was a regular customer and a heavy drinker, so she knew his face well. She screamed of course, but it was a busy night, noisy and raucous, and her screams weren't heard by those inside. The pirate held his hand over her mouth and then, to conceal his first murder, the pirate committed another.

'There in the back yard of her own inn, only a few feet from where her loving husband was laughing and pouring drinks inside, the innkeeper's wife was stabbed and stabbed and stabbed!'

Mary punctuated the word by slamming her fist repeatedly upon the arm of her chair. Paul jumped at the first bang, and hoped Nelia hadn't noticed.

'It was a brutal murder,' Mary shouted. 'As brutal as the first, because the pirate had learned to enjoy killing. Murderers always do, in the end. He dragged their bodies away in the night, but daylight revealed the victims' blood. There was blood everywhere, pooled on the ground, blood splashed and splattered and in drag marks across the stones and onto the sand, to the tideline where the murderer had pulled the bodies into the sea.

'The corpses washed up within a day or so. First the unknown sailor, who had been killed first. Then the Innkeeper's wife, easy to recognise in her long black dress, with her long black hair.

'The Innkeeper was heartbroken and desperate for justice, but nobody had any idea who had killed his wife or why. News of the confusion reached the murderer. At first, he had stayed away from the Smuggler's Inn. But as time went by the murderer realised that neither the authorities, nor the patrons of the inn, suspected him. He listened to the gossip, nodded and shrugged with other sailors who speculated about what might have happened, and eventually he began to feel safe. He began to feel so safe, in fact, that he decided it would look more suspicious if he *didn't* return to the inn, to drink with his friends and to carry on living as he had before. And so, one night, he entered the bar with his head held high. He expressed his sympathies to the Innkeeper with false compassion, greeted his friends jovially, and seated himself with a tankard full of ale. He congratulated himself silently for being cunning enough to get away with murder.

'That night his seat faced away from the stairs, and so when the candles burned blue, when the bar fell suddenly cold and silent, as men stopped speaking and stared, it took the murderer a moment to realise that something was wrong. He noticed that all eyes had turned to him. Men he had known for years began to back away from him, their eyes wide with horror, flicking from him towards the stairs behind him. Someone began to pray, and then he turned…

'Behind him on the stairs was the ghost of the innkeeper's wife. All dressed in black, her face a corpse behind her funeral veil, her eyes fixed upon him, and her finger pointing. For she had returned from beyond the grave to identify her killer. And all who saw her knew that he was guilty of the crime. The innkeeper saw and he cried out for vengeance. And vengeance was served! The murderer was hanged for his crimes.

'It was believed that this vengeance would satisfy the ghost. But a woman in black is a restless spirit, and down the dark years the ghost would appear on the stairs to point out those who had murdered and not been punished for their crimes. It is said that even now she appears, seeking vengeance against evil men. Even now, if a black-hearted murderer *dares* to set foot into the Old Smuggler's Inn, the ghost of the innkeeper's wife will appear. The room will fall dark and the candles will burn low, and standing upon the stairs, the woman in black will point to any man with the black heart of a murderer!'

A smattering of applause followed the end of the story, until people realised that Mary's face was taut with horror. Her hands held out to ward something away.

'Do you see her?' Mary cried. 'Do you see the Woman in Black?'

Paul turned as he heard other people beginning to whisper.

On the stairs, framed by lantern light, was a figure draped in black. Dark veils lifted in the breeze and the hint of face, deathly white with dark black eye sockets, could be made out. People scrambled back as the figure lifted one hand. The hand was stark and white and trembling, clawed in black, the pointed finger began to lower towards the bar.

Mary's cousin turned to see what everyone was looking at, visibly jumped and almost fell from his stool.

The woman in black upon the stairs spoke with a whisper, hoarse and deep, a single word:

'*Confess!*'

Christian shuddered visibly and his lip trembled.

'*Confesssss!*' The voice roared loud enough to make everybody jump.

'I didn't mean to!' the young man blurted out. 'It's not my fault! She just wouldn't stop complaining! She never stopped complaining!'

'*You killed your mother! Confesssss…*' the ghostly figure moaned.

'I did! I didn't mean to do it! But I did!' Christian stumbled from his stool, backing away from the tall and sinister figure and that pale, accusing finger. 'The knife was in my hand and then… then she was just lying there! There was so much blood!' He put his hands over his face and began to sob and shudder.

The woman in black put her hands on her hips.

'Will that do?' she asked in a very masculine voice.

'Oh yes,' said a man by the door crisply. 'That will certainly do. I couldn't ask for a clearer confession.'

'Happy to help!' said the woman in black in a voice that Paul recognised as belonging to his friend.

'Kemp?' Paul asked, amazed.

'What's happening?' Christian asked, looking from face to face as the lanterns were turned back up and two men approached him.

'What is happening, you simpleton,' Mary snapped. 'Is you just confessed to your mother's murder. Everybody knew you'd done it. Just needed a little proof. Thank you for being here *Connétable.*'

'Wouldn't have missed it,' the *connétable* gave Christian a shove towards the door, and swept a bow. 'Felicitations to the happy couple.'

'Glad to be of assistance,' said Mary with a hard smile. 'Now please, get Christian out of my sight, will you? I've got a husband to marry.'

'Kemp?' Paul said again as the woman in black lifted her veil and stomped to the bar. He rummaged within his false bosom and pulled out a pipe. His face was covered in white grease paint, his lips and eye sockets painted black.

'Can't believe that worked,' said Kemp, and accepted a drink with a nod to the barman.

'What would you have done if it hadn't?' Paul asked, beginning to laugh.

'Pretended it was a bad joke,' said Mary slapping him on the back.

'Sorry to anyone who got a fright!' She shouted. 'But there was no way we were letting that little worm have his mother's inheritance. Even if we did have to plan the most absurd wedding I ever heard of to trap him.'

Gabbon slipped an arm around her waist and told Paul. 'We have a man dressed as the Tchéziot in the woods too. Just in case. We were fairly certain Christian would give himself away at some point. After his brother got all scorched by that hell hound, he came over a bit superstitious.'

'Poor Aunt Catherine. She hated ghost stories,' Mary added.

Nelia shook her head in disbelief and laughed. 'And I suppose you have friends pretending to be ghouls in the graveyard?'

'No. We tried to get somebody to wait in an open grave and grab his ankle, but nobody would do it,' Mary admitted.

'Oh, nobody wanted to wait in an open grave in the darkness surrounded by dead people? I can't imagine why...' Nelia laughed again.

'So there never was a woman in black?' Paul demanded. 'You made up the story?'

'Oh no! There's a real legend right enough,' Gabbon said. 'But you can't rely on a ghost not to just take a night off. Besides, if people don't know the story, they'd just see a woman, standing on the stairs, pointing. Probably just assume she was a customer who'd had one too many.'

'Don't believe in ghosts,' Kemp said with a sour expression.

'Now drink up, will you?' Gabbon said. 'We've got to herd all these guests to the church.'

'*Drink up!*' Mary roared.

Within a few minutes a tipsy rag-tag wedding party had set out from the Smugger's Inn. A few people were carrying lanterns as they walked across the sand dunes towards woodland.

'Shame the tide's up. It's faster when you can just walk across the beach,' Gabbon said. 'The church is at the other end of the bay.'

Kemp was soon complaining that his dress was too tight and chafing under the arms. He stopped to tuck his skirts into his undergarments and fell behind. As the land began to rise and the group approached the tall pines that Mary had described as faery woods, the conversation became quieter. Shadows seemed to press in as trees reared up from the darkness and clusters of people fell into single file.

'So, these are the Faery Woods?' Nelia asked Gabbon. 'What's this area called?'

'*Pointe le Grouin.*'

'That's a pretty name,' she said. 'What does it mean in English?'

'Pig's snout.'

'Oh. Everybody's gone quiet. Are people actually scared?' Nelia asked quietly.

'Here?' Gabbon nodded. 'Yes! Faeries don't muck about in these islands. They're a powerful bunch. It would have been a much shorter walk to the church... if the fae hadn't *picked it up and moved it*. Stay on the path, Paul!'

'What was that thing called? The devil monster?'

'*Tchéziot,*' Gabbon said grimly, 'Even when I didn't much believe in evil Fae things, that creature scared me.'

The steps of the wedding party slowed and became more careful as people made sure to stay on the path. The people with lanterns lifted them high to spread the light and make sure the path was clear.

An unholy scream cut through the night, a raw shriek like metal on stone, a sound so horrible that Paul felt his stomach turn with dread and pulled Nelia close to him.

'It's an owl! It's just a barn owl!' Mary shouted, and shaky laughter broke out as someone lifted a lantern high enough to reveal a white bird in the low branches, its wings raised defensively.

'No point getting jumpy!' Gabbon said loudly. 'There's a man in a hood out here somewhere. He was waiting to jump out and scare Mary's cousin daft, so sooner or later he'll come swooping out of the night and give us all a scare.'

'Honestly we really didn't expect the woman in black thing to work,' Mary admitted.

They continued, almost in silence along the path, peering into the darkness of the woods, expecting a cloaked figure to loom from behind a tree at any moment. The longer they walked, the more tense it became. Kemp had managed to catch up, despite his ongoing battle with the dress. 'Where's the hooded man?' he asked. 'The suspense is making my skin crawl. Ghosts and faeries and monsters. I never should have agreed to be the Best Man.'

'Do you feel like something's watching us?' Nelia asked, and Paul took her hand.

'There's something out there in the trees,' Mary muttered. 'I can feel it. I never did like this island.'

The wedding guests walked swiftly in single file in the centre of the path. Slowly the land peaked and then began to descend. Tension was so high that when a cloaked figure stepped into the circle of light cast by Gabbon's lantern, people shouted and fell back, even though the black-clad assailant was already wringing its hands and apologising nervously. One woman screamed and tried to jump into her husband's arms, knocking him off balance and landing them both in a sprawl at Paul's feet.

'Where the bloody hell did you get to?' Gabbon demanded. 'Put that hood down, you fool.'

'I'm sorry, Uncle! I couldn't stay in the woods. It was so dark, and I *swear* there was something moving between the trees,' the lanky youth put the hood down to reveal a face pale with fear. 'I could hear something breathing, all rough like it was dying, and then there was this scream like nothing you ever …'

He trailed off as Mary waved her hands impatiently. 'It's fine, Pete. We got Christian with the ghost story anyway. Now come on, everybody. We're out of the wood. No more single file! Let's not keep the Reverend Edouard waiting.'

Conversation brightened with the easy walk towards the church, which was lit up prettily at the end of the bay. It had a high wall that curved around the graveyard. When they reached it, an iron-barred gate led inside. The wedding party again slowed their steps, each falling back in the hope that others would walk ahead of them.

'What now?' Mary demanded as Gabbon opened the gate for her and everyone else lingered.

'Is it true? About the ghouls?' somebody asked.

'How should I know?' Mary threw her hands in the air. 'Even if it is true, you'd have to be a killer to worry about them, wouldn't you?'

'I was a soldier,' Kemp said. 'Does that count?'

'I bloody hope not,' Gabbon muttered.

'I once sold a man an egg that gave him food poisoning and then he died, does that count?' The large woman asked from the shadows at the back of the wedding party. Then people started talking at the same time.

'I walked away from holding my friend's ladder when he was fixing his roof and –'

'I didn't know one of my sailors had fallen overboard in a storm, does–'

'Me and my brother pushed his friend into the harbour when we were drunk and didn't realise the tide was out–'

'Has *everybody* here killed someone?' Paul hissed in Nelia's ear.

'Quiet! Be quiet!' Mary shouted. 'I once sold a man a bottle of absinthe and the damned fool drank it all on the same night, then went mad, ran naked into the sea and was never seen again! Does that make me a killer? I don't know. What I *do* know is that the church I'm going to be married in is on the other side of this very pretty graveyard. So we will walk across it with no further fuss or nonsense! Ghouls? Who's sacred of a few ghouls? Whistle if you must, but we're going. Shall we go?'

Mary offered her hand to her fiancé.

'We shall indeed,' said Gabbon firmly, linking her arm with his as they set out.

All was still as they began walking. The wedding party began to file along the path with increasing confidence until white claws broke the surface of a grave. In the shadows around them the earth began to shift and displace like the surface of a pot beginning to bubble and boil. Something pale pulled itself out of the ground behind a gravestone and shook off ground like a dog shakes off water. A wet sound of sniffing sounded from the darkness. Other pale bodies began to crawl like maggots from beneath the ground.

'*Whistle! Start whistling!*' Nelia shouted.

The sound of discordant whistles in a dozen different tunes pierced the quiet graveyard.

'I can't think of a tune! Why can't I think of a tune?' Paul exclaimed.

There was hissing from the darkness and Paul caught sight of a ghoul stalking alongside the wedding party. He had expected it to look more human, but it had a hunched and bestial shape. Its powerful hindquarters were higher than its blunt, sightless muzzle, which was low to the ground. It was sniffing, snuffling like a pig. Saliva dripped and gleamed in the lantern light and its long tongue snaked out to taste the ground.

The wedding party shuffled and whistled, and got in its own way, as everybody tried their best not to be on the outside of the little stumbling crowd of people making their way down the narrow path.

'Is that Reverend Edouard? Why is he waving his arms?' Mary shouted. 'I can't hear him over all this damned whistling!'

As they got closer to the church everyone began to run and they arrived in a disorganised rush. The large lady with the large bonnet lost her bonnet and screamed when she saw a ghoul chewing on it. A man had lost half a trouser leg where a ghoul had grabbed him, but all the guests had made it across the graveyard relatively unharmed.

'What were you saying, Reverend?' Gabbon asked as whistling guests filed quickly into the church.

'I *said*, "go around", Gabbon. Why didn't you just go around? You can't go upsetting the ghouls at this time of night. We've just reseeded the grass. Come along inside. Quick now! Before one of them gets in and knocks over the font again.'

'*Promise* me our wedding day will be more normal than this,' Paul begged Nelia as Kemp held the door and they slipped inside.

Kemp ushered in the rest of the wedding party as a ghoul stalked slowly towards the entrance. It was the one that had been chewing on the large lady's bonnet. The ribbons had somehow become tangled around its neck, and the battered hat was dragging along as it advanced.

'Worst wedding disguise I've ever seen,' Kemp said. 'You don't fool me.'

He straightened his dress, stepped inside and firmly closed the heavy door behind him.

LES SYRAINES

ok wow… unfollowing now. was a big fan of their music but I was not aware they were using it to lure sailors to a watery grave by dashing their ships against the rocky coast of their island

@YuckyTom

A fisherman from Guernsey was at sea one day when he heard the sound of singing.

Constantin was an experienced man, who knew the stretch of sea between the coasts of Jersey and Guernsey could be treacherous. Yet he felt, like an ache in his heart, that he needed to hear more of the song being sung.

The wind blew from the south, carrying and then snatching away the song. He knew that he should return to shore with his catch, to his family and safety, yet a desperate curiosity made him change the sail and set his little boat towards the south. Tacking, slow and determined, he sailed towards the line of cliffs that marked the northern shore of Jersey.

He was an excellent sailor, and his little boat was swift. Before long he was passing the reef of rocks known as the Paternosters. Constantin shivered with the unnatural cold that always seemed to linger around these rocks. Cold death lingered there even on the warmest days. A cursed place that he usually avoided.

Yet the singing… sweet as a breeze against his neck on a hot day. A lover's sigh. It was intriguing, intoxicating, a sensuous harmony of two voices that became clearer as he sailed closer. There were words in it, he was certain, but the language was rich and strange, unlike any he knew of.

It was a duet of unspeakable beauty that spoke of something beyond the madness of obsession and the intoxication of desperate yearning. As music alters emotions, so Constantin found his feelings tangled and torn and wrenched to heights and depths he had never experienced. Such miraculous emotions, such agonising pleasure. He dropped his face into his hands, overwhelmed and barely able to contain what he felt. A song of hopeless need, with the promise of fulfilment.

They wove within their own echoes, these two singers, sounding the volume of their song against the cliffs. Their music rose and fell with the wind and the rhythm of the waves. It lingered in a way no natural sound could lay upon the air. There were moments when their reflected sounds and nature's rhythms formed a choir and chorus from the tumult, to create an ever-changing symphony.

The feminine voice was sweet and seductive as the whisper of the wind before a hurricane. The other lowered in flawless compliment, anticipating and combining. It was so beautiful that tears filled Constantin's eyes and emotion turned his hands to palsied shaking.

Their resonance of the song whispered over his skin like a lover's lips and hummed in his bones, flooding his mind with euphoria. The pleasure became almost painful.

He turned his boat towards the rocks in fumbling desperation, thinking only that he wanted to hear the singing more closely, more clearly. He could see the singers sitting at the foot of the cliffs.

The woman stood when she saw him, her hands lifted as though her fingers helped weave her voice into the air. She was luminous with pleasure, her white hair wild in the wind. Her dress was a diaphanous floating fabric, thin as ocean mist.

The young man was leaning back over a curve of rock, with his shirt open and his hands behind his head. His chin raised, his throat bared, one knee bent and his other foot swinging back and forth, idly keeping time. He looked absurdly languid as he created music that would make gods and kings fall to their knees.

They were pale as alabaster, these two singers, and elegant as dancers. They were predatory of gaze when they looked at him.

They must be brother and sister these two, Constantin thought, to look so strange and yet so similar to one another. He reached out a hand, tried to find the words to tell them how beautiful their song was to him. To explain to them that they made all other music he had ever heard sound as though it had been created by idiot children beating on buckets and screaming with self-important presumption.

He noticed someone else was there. Between the singers, his head in his hands, sat a young man with dark hair. Despite the astonishing beauty of the music surrounding him, his expression when he looked up was one of such raw grief that Constantin thought he must be somehow unaware of the song that resonated in the air.

The woman lifted to her tiptoes and danced, twirling to where the dark pebbles of a little cove met the sea and then stepped ankle deep into the rippling waves. The brother stood, his cropped white hair falling across his brow as he unfolded with easy grace.

'Welcome,' said the man, and his voice rang through Constantin's body as though it were a harp string plucked hard. He fell to his knees in the boat, shuddering with horrible pleasure then, as the pleasure fell away, he began trembling like a drunkard who had been roughly woken.

'A catch of a single little fish,' said the woman, and even her cruel little sneer made him twitch with pleasure.

'Don't listen to them,' said the man with the dark hair.

Constantin looked at him, almost shocked by the dull humanity of his voice. A soft Irish accent, flat with misery. Perhaps he might have been handsome were it not for the shadows like bruises beneath his eyes, and the contrast of his glorious companions and their impossible beauty.

'Don't be dull Brendan,' said the woman. 'You are so unoriginal these days.' She kicked a spray of seawater towards him, 'At least tell this little fisherman to take a knife and cut into his own ears. Tell him to run. Scream at him to swim, Brendan. Tell him to start screaming himself, until it drowns out our voices. Tell him all you want. They never listen, do they? None of you humans ever listen. Because you can't.'

She smiled at Constantin like a lover. His heart leapt in his chest as his enthralled mind tried to make sense of what she was saying. His concerns fluttered like feathers in the breeze and drifted away.

'This man must answer for his crimes,' the young man flicked his white hair from his eyes and smiled. His teeth were white, and neat and sharp. He crooked a finger and Constantin stumbled from his boat, fell and crawled up the dark shale beneath the cliffs until he could find his feet and climb onto the waist-high, flat, white rock where the pale man pointed.

'How do you not tire of this, Arian?' The man with the dark hair sounded anguished.

White hair whipped as brother and sister turned to glare at the Irish man.

'I am your *Prince*,' snapped Arian. 'You should address me with more respect if you value your life, Brendan.'

'Value my *life*?' Brendan let out a humourless laugh. 'Now why would I do that?'

Arian smiled a slow smile, then leapt elegantly onto the flat rock to stand opposite Constantin. His eyes were cold and blue as a winter sea.

'Kneel and be judged,' he intoned.

Constantin's legs buckled beneath him. A puppet with its strings cut could not have fallen faster. His teeth slammed together as he landed on his knees and bit his tongue. He winced, touched fingers to his mouth, and they came away bloody.

'Oh, you *poor* thing,' the woman reached up and grabbed his wrist with a grip of steel. She lifted his hand to her mouth. Constantin's breath caught in his chest as she tasted the blood on his fingers.

'Don't bite him, Selene,' said her brother irritably. 'I want him awake and aware.'

The woman pouted performatively then leaned closer to Constantin, tilting her head slowly as though she might kiss him. He felt her breath on his neck as her lips brushed his skin. Then beside his ear she whispered, softly, '*Wake up.*'

Clarity poured into his mind like iced water. It was a shock of sudden, unwanted sobriety. He felt abruptly woken from a strange and pleasant dream into a stranger, terrifying reality. Fear poured over him like icy water.

'What is happening? What did you do to me?'

He glanced from the sister to the brother and saw that they were enjoying his growing fear. Then he looked to the only other person that he was sure was human.

'You there! Brendan? What's happening?'

The dark-haired man glanced at him with a wince and then turned away, saying, 'Just close your eyes, my friend. It'll be over soon,' as his fingers plucked convulsively at the hem of his tattered shirt.

'Don't look at Brendan. Look at *me*. You *want* to look at me, don't you?' Arian's voice was like a cold hand turning Constantin's chin, a compulsion he could not ignore. The woman moved away and he could not even watch her go.

'You are accused of trespass to these isles,' Arian said. 'You are accused of theft. How do you answer these charges?'

'Theft?' Constantin squinted in confusion, 'I have stolen nothing from you. From you or anyone.'

'For God's sake, *your highness*,' Brendan said bitterly. 'He's just a fisherman.'

'Are the fish not mine?' The Prince demanded. 'Are these islands not mine?'

'If they are, sir,' Constantin said carefully. 'I did not know. I beg your forgiveness for any wrong I may have done you. Only tell me how I might make amends.'

'Oh, I like this one,' the Princess laughed.

'You cannot make amends,' the Prince said with a smile. 'Your crime was committed and you must be punished.'

'What crime?' Constantin tried to stand but his legs would not obey him. 'Look,' he tried to speak reasonably. 'I apologise if I have insulted you somehow, but I have done nothing wrong. I have committed no crime. A thousand other men fish these waters, what difference does it make if I catch a few?'

Arian grinned and Constantin noticed his teeth were sharp.

'It probably makes a difference to the fish,' Arian said. 'But who cares about a fish? And who cares about a fisherman?'

'He hasn't even heard of you! If you let him go,' Brendan said urgently, rising to his feet, 'he could tell so many others about you. The Sirens of Sorel! You both, my Prince, my Princess, could be wor-shipped like gods. You could be feared and desired by all mankind. The world would know your power and they would tremble!'

Arian threw back his head with a shout of laughter and then sighed. 'Perhaps one day my sister will let you go, and I won't have to listen to you fussing each time a ship of fools smashes themselves against our cliffs at the sound of singing.'

'Let him go?' Selene sank down beside Brendan and her voice slipped into a soft caress. 'But he doesn't *want* to go. He loves me, don't you Brendan?' She gripped his chin and snarled, *'Love me, Brendan.'*

Constantin watched Brendan's face change, a moment of struggle, from bitter despair to an expression of confused devotion.

'Of course I love you,' he said with absolute sincerity. 'I've *always* loved you. How could you ever doubt it?'

Arian snorted.

'*Remember*,' Selene whispered.

Brendan's expression of adoration faded, his handsome features twisted, and he recoiled and sat down abruptly. His tired gaze met Constantin's as he drew his legs to his chest and hugged them. 'I'm sorry,' he said and he turned his head away, resting it on his knees.

The Prince drew his sword slowly, indulgently, enjoying the soft ring of blade against scabbard, and the fisherman's fear as the cold metal was revealed.

'But I haven't *done* anything,' shouted Constantin.

The sword glinted and he strained muscles that would not respond. He found he could, at least, close his eyes.

'You are human,' said the Prince, his voice filled with loathing. 'That is crime enough.'

The blade whipped, swift and bright as a fish through water and hacked in one faultless strike through Constantin's neck. Blood spattered on the rock, as it had so many times before. Arian jumped down from the sacrificial stone as the fisherman's body collapsed.

'Why won't you just kill me?' Brendan asked quietly, without moving. 'How many more times must I see this? How many more years must I suffer this nightmare?'

Arian swept his sword through the ocean and the blood washed away. The pale metal never tarnished or rusted. It was forged from something ancient, that had never been wielded by human hands. A darker line of a duller metal decorated its length in exquisite filigree. The Prince admired it for a moment, watching it glint in the weak sunlight, then he re-sheathed it and smiled. He walked to where Brendan sat. He waited for the human to meet his eyes.

'I will kill you, Brendan, the moment you stop wanting to die.' He smiled. Then he stood and embraced the Princess who was scowling at him. He stroked her hair and placed a gentle kiss on her cheek.

'Don't worry, Selene,' he laughed. 'He will *never* stop wanting to die! Shall we sing again, my sweet sister? Let's see what else we might catch before the sun goes down.'

STORM WITCHES

The storme will arise,
And trouble the skies;
This night, and more for the wonder

Robert Herrick

'What are you looking for Norah?' Hubert called to his daughter.

His daughter glanced back at him from the rail of the boat, then narrowed her eyes towards the horizon again.

'Pirates,' she said in a grim voice.

'Pirates?' Hubert turned to where his wife stood at the tiller, her dark hair whipping in the breeze, and asked, 'Madelaine, my love, have you been reading Norah that Walter Scott novel again?'

Madelaine considered the question for a moment, repressed a smile, and said, 'No. I haven't been reading it to her, Hu.'

Hubert smiled and nodded. 'I see. Let me rephrase the question then. Did you give Norah the book to read by herself?'

Madelaine grinned back and then shrugged apologetically. 'Oh in *that* case, yes, I did.'

Hubert sighed. 'It's all very well, *mon vie*, but you know that now Norah has pirates in her head, she'll panic every time she sees another ship.'

'On the upside,' his wife pointed out, 'in the *very* unlikely event that there ever were any pirates, we'd certainly know about it in good time. And we have a magnificently literate eight-year-old child, which is a very rare thing, you know.'

Madelaine smiled proudly at Norah, who was fair like her father. Her long blonde plait was coming undone, and she had lost her ribbon.

'It's not that I'm not proud of her, Madelaine,' Hubert said. 'I just wish we could find her some books about little faeries or something.'

Madelaine pulled a face. 'Any stories she hears about faeries in *this* island might terrify her to death. Oh, for goodness sake, no, Norah!' Madelaine gave her husband a little shove. 'Stop her, Hu! She's trying to climb the mast again.'

Hubert took two steps, swept his daughter into a hug and assured her that there wouldn't be any pirates this close to land.

Madelaine shouted so her voice was not stolen by the wind. 'As far as I remember, Norah, all the old stories of pirates around Jersey happened to the *west* of the island.'

Hubert nodded. 'Your mother is right, and that's the other side of Jersey. We're just coming around the *east* coast, towards Green Island, do you see it there with the grass on top? We're heading for La Rocque harbour. Besides! Pirates only attack at night and in storms, when the wind blows the boat like this!'

Hubert spun his daughter around in circles until she screamed with delight.

'Your father's right,' Madelaine laughed. 'There won't be pirates on sunny days like this. So stop worrying. Look how pretty the island is here! Hu will you take the tiller for a moment, I want to put on a shawl.'

'We're heading just around those rocks sticking out on the coast ahead and we'll be in sight of the harbour,' Hubert assured his daughter as he stepped away to take the tiller. 'We're *almost* home and safe on dry land!'

He lowered his voice as he leant near his wife and whispered, 'It's not pirates that worry me, around here. Sailing past... *that place...* always puts me on edge.'

Hubert jutted his chin towards the land. Madelaine studied the coastline and compressed her lips, her easy smile fading.

'It's been a very long time, Hubert. We've never heard anything about them since.' She shot him a quick grin and added, 'Anyway, I don't think you ever had much to worry about. They liked *you* just fine.'

'*Nothing* to worry about?' Hubert snorted. 'Having my mind enchanted until I didn't know who I was, or what I wanted. I could have lost the woman I love. I'd say *that* was something to worry about! And they scared the bloody life out of me.'

Hubert stared grimly at the rocks as they approached. 'They might have seemed kind for a little while, but for all we know, they may have been planning to drown me. Or eat me.'

'I rather think they had *other* things in mind.'

'Who had what in mind?' Norah asked as she ran over.

'Why are you only ever listening when I don't want you to?' Madelaine demanded fondly.

'Yes, but who are you talking about?' Norah asked, staring up at her with interested blue eyes.

'Were talking about witches, love.' Hubert gently tugged her plait.

'Hu!' Madelaine scolded. 'I can't believe I get told off for letting her read a storybook about pirates, and you're telling her about witches!'

'I didn't *tell* her anything! Anyway, Norah, it's just an old legend, about a big rock where witches would sit and ask fishermen for fish. You'll see it in a minute. I'll point it out.'

'Will we see witches?' Norah demanded.

Madelaine smiled and pulled Norah into a quick hug, saying, 'No, Norah. Daddy met some witches about ten years ago, but it's nothing to worry about.'

'Witches aren't real,' Norah said. 'Dad said so when the men killed that old lady, remember? *Pirates* are real though.'

'You told her witches aren't real?' Madelaine whispered as their daughter dashed forward to the prow. '*You*, of all people, told her that witches aren't real?'

Hubert laughed. 'You know what I meant. All those poor people that get accused of witchcraft, when they're just making a poultice, or using herbs. *People* aren't witches, is what I was trying to tell Norah. I don't want her getting superstitious and thinking somebody she meets is a witch, just because they've got warts or a squint. Everyone's gone bloody mad. There's always some poor woman being accused for something ridiculous.'

'Like having a cat. Or living alone. Or sneezing on a Sunday.'

As they passed Green Island, the perfect blue of the sea was troubled by a rippling breeze that was raking its shining surface into choppy little peaks. Hubert and Madelaine both eyed the land ahead. Through the trees on the shore, they could just make out a high rocky outcropping of russet granite. The place known as Rocqueberg.

As Hubert hauled on a rope, the wind changed direction completely and the boom swung around so fast he had to duck.

'Careful, Hu!' Madelaine exclaimed. 'I'm glad we're nearly home. Can you take the tiller again? The current is too strong for me.'

The muscles in Hubert's arm stood out as he began to fight to hold the tiller steady. While their daughter watched the horizon to starboard for pirates, Madelaine and Hubert's glances flicked again and again towards the land.

'Nearly home,' Hubert muttered again.

Madelaine grabbed her coat as the wind grew colder. The blue sky above had turned misty white. The wind changed again, slowing them, and they became uncertain how to set their sail, as the wind blew first one way and then another. The boom swung back and forth, and Norah crouched down nervously as her parents fought to keep the boat on course. The water seemed to swirl as erratically as the breeze. Norah crawled over to grab her cardigan and then announced loudly that she had left her hat in France. The sky grew darker while the ship made little progress.

Hubert's fists clenched suddenly around the rope he was pulling, and he froze. Madelaine looked at him curiously. When his eyes met hers, there was fear in them.

'What's wrong?' Madelaine demanded, but a gust of wind stole her words. Hubert pointed to his ear and then to the sky as the rope fell slack from his hands.

Madelaine listened. For a long moment she heard nothing except the wind. Then she caught it – it sounded so much like a whisper behind her ear that she spun around.

'*Thirteen…*'

Then the wind began to roar.

Norah's plait lifted and lashed behind her, strands of hair whipping around her startled face as she grabbed onto the rail. The boat leaned low to the water, suddenly speeding forward towards the rocks. Ropes strained as though they would snap.

'Lower the sail!' Madelaine shouted, and Hubert nodded.

They struggled to release ropes and lower the canvas. The rigging fell loose around them. The boat lost momentum and floundered, dipping and rocking from side to side. The sky was growing darker.

'*Your thirteenth is ours!*'

The whisper in the wind seared Madelaine's ears so loudly that she gasped. Norah let out a little cry and sunk to the deck in fear. Hubert hugged her as a wave lifted the boat and pushed it with a lurch in the direction of the shore. The boat fell from the back of the wave's peak with a stomach-churning dive. Then another huge wave hit them. They spun around, pressed helplessly against the rails.

The sky darkened like night was falling as heavy storm clouds gathered and pressed down. A single flash of lightning blinded them, thunder roared, and within a moment it was raining as hard as if they had sailed beneath a waterfall.

Storms at sea often began fast and unexpectedly, but this was like nothing the couple had ever experienced. Madelaine's clothes were soaked within seconds. Shapes twisted in the rain as something invisible stirred in the drops, and the hissing of water hitting the deck picked up the word *thirteen* and turned it to a repetitive roar. The rain came down so hard Madelaine could barely make out the shape of her husband and child. The deck shifted beneath her feet, and she slid from one side of the boat to the other.

'*Mum!*' Norah's shout made Madelaine crawl towards her husband and daughter who were hunched against the starboard rail. She wrapped her left arm around Hubert's back and grabbed the rail tight with Norah clasped between them. The boat heaved high upon a wave and tipped to the right. Madelaine saw the sea lunge towards them with sickening speed, before the ship righted itself and began to spin, so swiftly that the land seemed to dance around them, so dizzying that Madelaine had to close her eyes.

When the ship finally slowed, Madelaine saw what she had most dreaded to see. Dark figures were standing on the rocks of the shore. They were silhouettes against a deep grey sky and beneath the trees.

The Witches of Rocqueberg.

'There's a lot more witches than last time, Hu,' Madelaine said, her hand clutched his shirt so hard she thought her fingernails might tear through. 'Hubert, there's *so many* of them!'

Something white blew past the mast, too fast to see, and Madelaine's wet hair whipped into her eyes. A wave arced above the deck. A woman's shadow curved within the water. As the wave crashed onto the deck the water reformed. It grew into a glittering, moving statue. The shape of a woman made of water. She looked at them with a cold smile, then ran to the rail, steps glittering with diamond drops, before diving back into the ocean.

'Mum, did you see her?' Norah shouted.

'I know, Norah. Don't look at them.' Madelaine tried to cover her daughter's eyes.

'No! Please, mum. I want to see!'

Waves pushed them relentlessly towards the black rocks that marked the shore. The boat lurched towards the shadowy figures gathered there. The rain was relenting as swiftly as it had started.

'*Thirteenth.*'

The Witches spoke the words together and the sound was echoed in the wash of the waves and the gusts of the air.

'That old tale,' Hubert's voice was rough with fear. 'In the legend the Witches would do this to fisherman trying to make their way home. They used to demand the thirteenth fish from the catch as a toll before they would let them pass.'

'I remember,' Madelaine said.

'Do you happen to remember what happened if the fishermen hadn't caught thirteen fish?'

Madelaine stared at him blankly.

'Well, Dad?' Norah asked Hubert. 'What happened?'

'Nothing good, I imagine,' said Madelaine slowly.

'But we don't *have* any fish,' Norah pointed out.

'That could be a problem.' Hubert bit his lip.

They looked towards the land. A wave crashed against the rocks, and from the receding white water the shapes of sleek, gleaming women slithered and climbed ashore. Figures as pale as clouds blew in like torn cloth, spun, and formed into human shapes like smoke blown into invisible glass as they alighted in easy crouches. Lightning flashed and a fire blazed into being beside the huge red rock of Rocqueberg. Female shapes danced from the depths of the flames, arms raised, hair whipping. The earth beneath the trees erupted in tangles of roots and brambles that clawed upwards and wove themselves into what looked like grotesque, tangled puppets, that stumbled, then gained in grace with every step. They dusted the earth and leaves from their skin, then stood with their hair lifting in the wind.

'*Your thirteenth fish.*'

The voices were a chorus.

'It must be *every* Witch in the islands!' Hubert swore and Madelaine half-heartedly covered Norah's ears. The boat grated against the rocks of the shore and the little family tumbled to the centre of the deck with the impact. Hubert held onto Madelaine and Norah, cushioning their fall as best he could.

'*Ow*,' Norah said, rolling over and rubbing her arm as she sat up.

Rock scratched the hull as witches with fingers of sharp stone anchored them in place.

'Please,' Hubert clambered to his feet as Madelaine knelt protectively in front of Norah. 'Please. We're not fishermen, but I am a fisherman's son. I promise, if you let us make our way to the harbour, I will buy nets and I will put back out to sea and I will catch you as *many* fish as you like. For as long as you like! Just please don't hurt my family.'

Madelaine slapped at him. 'Hubert! Don't make offers of *lifelong service* to fée creatures! What are you *thinking*?'

'The thirteenth fish of your catch.'

It was a single voice this time. A woman with golden hair and a voice as light as a breeze stepped forward from the crowd. 'The thirteenth fish, or risk our wrath. You know how this works, don't you, fisherman's son? For centuries that has been the toll for fishermen to pass our rock. *The thirteenth fish...* or we raise the storm and wreck your little boat.'

Madelaine narrowed her eyes at the blonde Witch.

'You can *clearly* see we have no fish!' she said. 'All we have is our daughter.'

'I'll catch you fish! *Any* number of fish!' Hubert said.

'Oh stop, Hu!' Madelaine clambered to her feet. 'They don't even *want* fish. They just want an excuse to cause chaos.'

Hubert turned and stared at her in horror.

'Madelaine, for goodness' sake, please don't anger them!'

'Why not?' Madelaine stood up, peeled off her soaking coat and threw it on the deck. 'If they're really going to sink our ship and risk murdering our daughter, then I'm not going to my watery grave without telling them *exactly* what I think of them!' She wrung out her dark hair, flicked it over her shoulder and glared up at the witches defiantly.

Norah suddenly called up to the Witches, 'Why do you *want* a thirteenth fish?'

'Shh, sweetheart, please,' Hubert said.

The blonde Witch tilted her head and answered the child's question. 'It is the toll,' she said. 'It has *always* been the toll. Even for old friends.'

Hubert and Madelaine exchanged worried glances.

'Yes, but *why?*' Norah tried to step around her mother. 'If you can change the weather and move the sea like this, then why do you need fishermen to catch you a fish? Surely you can catch your own fish.'

'It is the toll.' A woman, dripping with water, tilted her head. 'It has *always* been the toll.'

'Yes, but *why?*' Norah insisted.

'My daughter raises a good point,' Madelaine said crossing her arms. 'Why is it that you *absurdly* powerful women need some poor terrified fishermen to give you a sodding fish anyway?'

'It is the toll.' A woman with leaves in her hair had a voice like the creaking of trees in the wind.

'We heard that part,' Madelaine said patiently. 'Since we don't have a thirteenth fish, or any fish at all, we cannot pay the toll. Will you at least let my daughter out of the boat before you do whatever it is that you're going to do to us?'

'What if we had thirteen of something else instead though?' Norah asked, tilting her head to one side.

There was a strange synchronicity of movement as every witch turned their heads to look at the child.

'Well?' Hubert asked, desperately. 'What if we *did* happen to have thirteen of something else? Would that work? Because I think we might as it happens!'

Hubert was suddenly in motion, dragging luggage and crates from where they had been tightly lashed to the deck. He revealed a trapdoor that had previously been carefully concealed.

'What if we had something *better* than a fish?' Madelaine asked hopefully, 'How about that? Would that work?'

'You're really pretty,' said Norah to the wind witch.

The Witch twirled in the air and smiled, 'Thank you, child. I know. Thirteen of *what?*' she asked, swirling closer, curious.

With a jangle and a thump Hubert lifted out a crate of bottles and shoved them across the wet deck.

'Ladies!' Hubert held a bottle up like a salesman. 'Behold the finest cognac! All the way from France! Take *all* of it if you like. Just please, let our daughter go.'

'I hate it,' Norah said with ill-timed honesty. 'It's absolutely disgusting.'

'It's not disgusting, and you shouldn't have tried it,' Madelaine said firmly. 'Brandy isn't for children. Hubert did you give our child brandy?'

'Of course I didn't! She took a sip at the vineyard before I could stop her.'

The Witches drew closer. Those in the air floated like spirits. Two watery hands reached up from the sea, and a curious water witch poured herself onto the deck. She stood and looked at the crates and bottles, at the honey-amber liquid inside squat bottles packed in straw.

'Do you have *thirteen* bottles?' she asked pointedly.

'Yes! Yes? Hu, do we?' Madelaine asked.

Hubert began to pull out more crates, saying, 'I'm sure we do. One dozen to sell and the bottle we got for ourselves. I'm afraid I'm not sure which one would be the thirteenth though, so–'

'*That one.*' A watery hand pointed. '*That is the thirteenth bottle.*'

'How can you tell?' Hubert asked. 'We bought them all at the same time.'

'The thirteenth always glitters with a little dark magic,' the wind witch said with a smile.

'I should warn you,' said Madelaine. 'If one of those fire witches touches that bottle, it's going to explode like a cannonball.'

Another water witch poured onto the deck and stood up. She lifted the thirteenth bottle in her hand and looked questioningly to the other witches.

'Take as many as you want,' Hubert said holding two bottles out to the witches on the shore. 'It's a small payment for the lives of my family.'

'No. The toll is paid.' A woman with claws of stone released the boat and the others stepped back, looking suddenly more human.

The wind witch nodded and fluttered to the earth. The water witch who held the bottle smiled. In the time that it took her to run three swift steps, skip over the rail, and land on the shore, she had turned into a normal girl with black hair, dressed in damp trousers and a white shirt. She looked every inch a fisherman's daughter.

Norah ran after her to the rail and asked, 'How do they do that? I wish I could change like that!'

'No you don't,' Hubert said firmly.

The wind witch laughed and raised a farewell hand before turning and running in bare feet after the girl with the bottle. A gentle wave lifted the boat and pulled them back from the land.

'Is that it?' Hubert asked.

'Don't question good luck, Hubert. Set the sail before they change their insane, fickle minds.'

'Right! Yes,' Hubert jumped to help untangle ropes and hoist a sail, while Norah watched the witches from the rail.

'I like them,' Norah decided.

'No you don't, Norah!' her father said. 'Untangle that rope, Sweetheart, we're in a bit of a mess here.'

Madelaine grabbed the tiller, and said, 'Hubert, if they get absolutely legless and start a typhoon, they could destroy half the island.'

'If that happens, I promise to feel absolutely dreadful about it,' Hubert said. 'We'll worry about that later. We escaped with our lives *and* our boat, and that's good enough for me.'

The sail caught the breeze and their little boat surged forward over the calm sea towards La Rocque harbour.

Norah ran and stared towards the horizon and then shouted, 'Mum? Who do you think would win in a fight between pirates and witches?'

LES LOUPS-GAROUS

'Tis then the woods forsaking,
Their way cross country taking,
Nine howling wolves come hungering for food.
Aleksey Konstantinovich Tolstoy.

Matchi awoke in the deep hours of the night, restless and unsettled, to the sound of howling.

Silvery moonlight was creeping through the curtains. The boy got up to look out across the forested side of La Brecquette Manor. The moonlight painted the trees of L'Etacq forest silver and branches stirred in the rising wind, but the landscape was warped by the window, which was made of thick little diamonds of leaded glass. As Matchi pulled back the curtain and sat on the window seat, a movement caught his eye.

There was something at the edge of the trees. It stood upright, like a man, but had the look of a savage beast. Its limbs were long and powerful, its shoulders broad and covered with thick fur. Then it turned and was swallowed by the shadows beneath the trees. It had only been in sight for a moment, but it had turned its head before it slipped away. Matchi felt certain that it had seen him, and there was a malevolence in its gaze that filled his veins with ice.

The boy retreated, shivering in the darkness, to his bed.

Matchi hated the isolated family manor. His father had sent him here, from London, to convalesce, much against Matchi's own wishes, as soon as the doctor had deemed him well enough to travel by sea.

La Brecquette Manor was two stories high, built of granite, with a walled courtyard enclosing the stables and kitchen garden. There was a small chapel attached to the main house, which had a decorative steeple and a bell. On Sundays a few men and women would gather from the nearby fishing village for mass.

On the opposite side of the manor was the sea. At low tide the ocean retreated a quite astonishing distance, leaving desolate grey sand and dark rocks. At high tide the waves were so close that they seemed to crash against the walls. Matchi could hear them, whispering and roaring, while La Brecquette Manor stood like the prow of an unmoving ship.

When he awoke late the next morning Matchi briefly wondered if he had dreamed the monster, but his curtains were still half open as he had left them, and he felt as unsettled as he had the night before. He dressed and descended from his rooms, seeking human company. He found the housekeeper, Mrs Gavey, in the kitchen with her daughter Colette.

Matchi informed them, with the bland self-indulgence only an invalid could get away with, that he would be taking his breakfast in the kitchen where they might keep him company. Mrs Gavey scolded him fondly over the sound of boiling water while Colette busied herself at the sink. The blustering wind set doors and shutters rattling, and somewhere an unfastened gate was crashing open and closed. Above all the other noises a sharp high note kept sounding, so piercing that it made Matchi's head hurt. He could not imagine the source, and at length it annoyed him so much that he put his hands over his ears and demanded, 'Good lord what is that ringing sound? How do you stand it?'

'Do you mean the silver bell in the chapel, Master Wallis?'

'Is it really silver? Does it clatter and ring like that every time the wind blows wild? You must hate it!'

The housekeeper laughed and told him that the silver bell was the pride of the congregation but could not tell him why his forbears had chosen to have it cast in silver. She advised him to ask his father when he returned, and Matchi grumbled that his father was already two days late returning to Jersey.

The sound of the bell grated on his nerves so much that he climbed upstairs to the room nearest the chapel to stare at it. He watched it swinging and ringing in the gusts. It was no bigger than a tankard, and the metal was so dulled and tarnished by the sea air that Matchi doubted if it was silver at all.

His head ached and he began to feel exhausted. He wondered how anyone was supposed to recuperate in this lonely place, with its ceaseless wind and piercing bell and dogs that howled in the forest at night.

He began a letter to his father to communicate these sentiments, trying not to sound petulant or childish. He was not happy with how unsteady his penmanship looked, but he hoped his handwriting would be taken as carelessness, rather than the shaking that still troubled him after even the briefest exertions. He did not mention his sighting of the moonlit beast, for fear that his father would think him feverish again, or hysterical, which would only guarantee longer incarceration at La Brecquette manor. He gave the letter to Colette to post.

He need not have bothered, because the next day brought his father's ship with the tide. The shouting of sailors, and the noise of barrels and crates being unloaded onto the dock, woke him from an exhausted afternoon sleep. Before he could put on his boots there was a knock at his door. He opened it in bare feet, with his shirt untucked, expecting his father.

'Jane!' he shouted in delight.

His sister was pulling off her travelling cloak. Her cheeks were rosy, her blonde hair was in disarray, and she smelled of salt sea air.

'Brother dear, your letters were so miserable and pathetic that I thought I had better come and keep you company. You made La Brecquette Manor sound so grim and forbidding that I decided it must be positively romantic!' She drew her gloves off and slapped him playfully on the shoulder with them.

Matchi, laughing, wrapped his older sister in a hug and danced her around his room.

'How long will you stay?' he asked.

'For as long as you do, Matchi. I don't know what father was thinking leaving you alone here. Now, get dressed, will you? I'm hungry.'

They took tea in the drawing room and Matchi demanded to know where his father had disappeared to.

'Oh, Matchi, it's rather horrible,' Jane said, putting down her cup. 'The wife of one of the sailors saw the boat coming in and she met us at the dock. It seems their daughter has gone missing from the village.

Father has taken the crew to help with a search. You did not mention there was a village, Matchi. You made it sound like there was nothing for miles.'

'Jane, beyond the confines of the manor I can tell you nothing of this island *at all*. I am forbidden to go outside, for goodness sake! Do you think father would let us help search in the forest?'

'We are, I am afraid, instructed to remain inside.'

Matchi sighed and pushed his cup away, saying, 'No doubt father will continue to insist that this wretched sea air is beneficial. Although, how sea air could be beneficial to me when I am confined to the house is anyone's guess.'

'Well, you do look a *little* better to me, Brother.' Jane reached for his hand across the table and said, 'Matchi, just do as father tells you and he *may* relent. If you argue with him, he will only grow more stubborn. You know how he is. He only let me come here because I swore to be your nursemaid. So, we shall pretend to be quite dull. Eventually he will let you come home.'

As night began to fall, the brother and sister sat together on Matchi's window seat. They saw the lanterns of the search party spread further outwards from the village and through the forest, which stretched from the manor to the high hill beyond. As the tide receded, the lights began to slowly spread out across the beach and rocks that were revealed by the low tide.

'They must think she is drowned. I fear this has become a resigned and hopeless search.' Jane sighed. 'Go to bed, Matchi, before father comes home and finds you awake at this hour.'

Matchi's father, John Wallis, woke him in darkness to bid him farewell. The candlelight threw him into shadow as he sat and rested a cool hand on Matchi's brow.

'I don't have a fever, father,' Matchi said sleepily, trying to sit up. 'I'm quite well now, you know. Did you find the child?'

His father's profile was grim as he said, 'We didn't I'm afraid, Matchi. And it seems she's not the first person to go missing from the village in recent times. They're a superstitious lot though, so it's hard to get any sense out of them. They're talking about wolves in the forest. There haven't been wolves in this island for a century! I haven't woken Jane, so tell her I said goodbye.'

His father stood.

'I'm sailing with the tide, but I'll be back within the week, Matchi. Hopefully the girl will have turned up safe and sound by then. Go back to sleep, Son. I'll be back before you know it.'

Matchi found his sister yawning at breakfast and told her what his father had said.

'Well,' Jane answered, 'there may not be wolves but there was *something* howling in the woods last night. I wish the villagers would keep their wretched mongrels tied up. They woke me twice.'

'Honestly Jane, there have been nights I have lain awake wishing to throw those dogs in sacks and pay their passage to France, the damnable creatures.'

Jane laughed as she reached for an apple, then frowned.

'You won't heal if you can't sleep, Matchi.'

'Wait until the silver chapel bell starts ringing in the wind. Then you'll *truly* understand why I loathe this place,' said Matchi as he cracked the top of a boiled egg.

'A *silver* bell?' Jane asked.

'So I'm told. It gives out these long, high-pitched notes that one cannot ignore.'

After breakfast Matchi showed Jane around the house. They looked out at the chapel bell and debated whether it was truly silver.

Jane remarked that no matter how much Matchi disliked it, she thought La Brecquette rather a fine place, with its rosy granite and dark oak. As the days passed his sister was continually astonished by the changes in the sea. Not just the extremes of the tide, but how it could be calm and blue as a topaz one hour, then a roaring hell of dark churning waves and white horses the next. They spent their time playing cards, reading, gossiping and bickering, and Jane decided that Matchi must be allowed some fresh air and exercise. They walked in the woods a little, and visited the beach, but Matchi still tired easily, so Jane would not let him go far. One stormy evening, when the bell had chimed twice and Jane had pleased her brother by agreeing that the sound was, indeed, very piercing, and very irritating, Matchi told his sister about the creature that he had seen on the night before she arrived.

'Perhaps it was just a nightmare?' Jane suggested.

Matchi shook his head and assured her that it was not, 'It was certainly not a wolf either, even though the villagers claim to have seen them.'

Jane laid her cards down and rubbed her eyes sleepily. 'If there *are* truly wolves in the forest it would explain the howling. I tasked Mrs Gavey with finding out who owns a dog in the village, but nobody will confess to it.'

A chorus of howling woke Matchi that night, and the sounds were closer than they had ever been before. He met Jane in the corridor as she burst from her room with a lantern in her hand.

'There's strange creatures out there, Matchi!' She said urgently. 'What if they get inside?'

'We must check the doors!' Matchi shouted.

They ran downstairs, their bare feet swift, checking everything was secure and locked. Matchi caught brief glimpses of movement through the windows, as the sound of howling echoed through the mansion. When all the doors were locked and the casements were closed, the siblings found each other again by the main stairs. They crept together, towards the old map room, which looked out towards the forest.

'Set down the lantern so they don't see the light,' Matchi whispered.

Jane left it in the corridor as they peered around the doorway towards the heavy, leaded windows and the scattered movements beyond.

'*Are* those wolves?' Jane whispered. 'What's *wrong* with them?'

Matchi saw the leaping wolf a brief second before it hit the casement.

In a deafening explosion of glass, it arced through the window, shattering wood and twisting metal. It landed in a tangled, bloodied sprawl on the map table. Its claws tore lines in the floorboards as it fell to the floor in the sliding debris and parchments.

Jane hauled Matchi from the room by his arm as the malformed wolf staggered to its feet and shook itself violently. Then she slammed shut the door. Both of them leant their backs against it as the thing on the other side clawed and snarled and barged against the wood. The door was heavy, solid oak, two inches thick. Jane noticed the key sitting in the lock and turned it.

'Let's go up to father's study. It's like a fortress!' Matchi whispered.

He pulled Jane to her feet. She grabbed the lantern, and they ran upstairs.

'Was it one of those things that you saw that night?' Jane asked.

'No, what I saw was similar, but bigger, and it stood upright. I can see why the villagers would think these things were wolves but...'

'That was not a wolf!'

They locked themselves in their father's study, watching through the upstairs window until the twisted, bestial shapes crept away into the forest. They finally fell asleep on the rich rug with only Jane's dressing gown for a blanket.

Matchi woke with a jump the next morning when his sister shook him. Morning light was creeping through the window shutters, but Jane had her fingers to her lips. 'Something's in the house!' she said softly into his ear.

He could hear sounds of movement on the lower floor. A door banged, then there were footsteps and the creaking of the stairs. Matchi reached for his sister's hand, and they exchanged a nervous glance.

'Miss Jane? Master Matchi?' A voice called.

'Good grief, it's just the housekeeper arrived from the village!' Jane exclaimed, relief clear in her tone. 'Matchi, help me move the desk away from the door.'

The housekeeper led the two young people downstairs to the kitchen. She set to making them breakfast. Chalk-faced she listened to them tell their story of the wolf creatures. Her daughter Colette came in as they were speaking, carrying a bucket of water from the spring. She was as pale as her mother and Jane remarked upon it. In defiance of convention, both mother and daughter sat down at the table with Matchi and Jane while they ate. They told how they too had hidden the night before, in their cottage with the shutters closed, peering through the slats. Things half-seen and terrifying had raced through the fishing village. They had heard screams and smelled smoke. In firelight they had glimpsed what they first thought were mad dogs. Swift monsters, silhouetted in smoke and fire, had attacked anyone who dared leave their homes. When dawn broke, Mrs Gavey and Colette had emerged to see one of the cottages burned to the ground. Doors on two more of the houses had been torn from their hinges, and seven people were missing.

'They aren't dogs, and they aren't wolves,' Jane said firmly, wrapping her fingers around her mug.

The housekeeper stood.

'Perhaps they are rabid. I don't believe it will be safe here, or in the village, tonight. Fortunately, my husband is due back from sea today. Pack some essential things, children. As soon as my husband is home, we'll come back for you. We'll head for the port at St Aubin's, where we will be safe.'

'Thank you, Mrs Gavey,' said Jane. 'We are most grateful. Well, Matchi, it seems you will have your wish to leave La Brecquette Manor after all!'

'The sooner the better,' Matchi said.

'We should be long gone before nightfall,' Mrs Gavey assured him.

Another storm was rising as Mrs Gavey left with her daughter. Matchi and Jane packed a few clothes, and waited, but the housekeeper did not return.

'What if Mr Gavey doesn't make it back to port?' Matchi asked uneasily as rain struck the windows, 'The weather is getting worse.'

'Then we'll lock ourselves in father's study for another night,' Jane smiled and squeezed his hand.

The afternoon drew on and the storm and sea continued to rise. Dark clouds swept in from the horizon throwing the house into gloom, and thunder was grumbling in the distance.

'You just wait until you see a storm here at high tide,' Matchi said gloomily.

'I'd rather not,' Jane said.

They sat together on the window seat in Matchi's bedroom, looking out along the path until Matchi began to yawn and Jane forced him to lay down and rest.

He jerked awake in a panic to see the house was even darker than it had been before. The wind was blustering around the house and Jane looked worried.

'I thought it best you rested, but it's almost night, Matchi. Even if they come now, we can't leave and risk being out in the open. There are waves breaking over the dock and flooding up as far as the gate. Perhaps we should go to father's study *now*.'

Matchi agreed and they quickly collected a few things for the night. Jane carried a jug of water and a lantern. Matchi grabbed a tray with bread and cheese. Jane seated herself at the study window while Matchi ate, until a flash of lightning lit the trees, showing the forest in stark, bright monochrome.

'Someone's out there!' Jane exclaimed.

Matchi stood beside her at the window, but the darkness was almost complete. Moonlight was blocked by storm clouds. The rising wind rattled the shutters in a gust that made the trees seem to lean away from the ocean. Thunder roared, and another lightning flash revealed the housekeeper and her daughter racing up the forest lane towards the courtyard gates, waving desperately up at the window. Jane stopped Matchi with a firm hand on his arm.

'Let them come up to us,' she said. 'Mrs Gavey has a key.'

They met the two servants at the top of the stairs. The women looked frantic, their clothes and hair in disarray as they raced upwards, their eyes wild in the lantern light.

'Quickly! They're coming!' The housekeeper whispered.

The siblings rushed them to the study and closed the door behind them. Matchi ran to the window. Another stuttering flash of lightning lit the unnatural shapes of long-limbed wolves racing through the forest towards La Brecquette Manor.

Jane was struggling to push their father's desk back against the door on her own. Waves boomed on the other side of the house, but it was another sound that caught Matchi's attention.

'What is that banging?' he asked in alarm. 'Did you leave the front door open? Dear God, are you *mad*?'

The housekeeper's daughter began to laugh and then, as the wind gusted and the silver bell rang out, she screamed. Both mother and daughter crumpled as though struck and covered their ears with their hands. Their limbs contorted and their faces twisted.

'What's wrong with them?' Jane cried.

Matchi staggered back from them as their jaws cracked and distorted and their teeth grew into fangs.

'Jane,' Matchi whispered, gripping his sister's arm, 'they're monsters!'

'And we let them inside. Help me, Matchi, we have to get out!'

They ran to drag the table aside from the door, but the thing that had been Mrs Gavey slammed a clawed hand down upon the desk. She held it steady with shocking strength. Colette had fallen to the floor, bones cracking and reshaping. Jane picked up her father's letter-opener, a delicate little silver blade, and stabbed the housekeeper's clawed hand with all her strength.

The woman opened her mouth to scream, and a ragged roar issued from her throat. She ripped her hand back, tearing her own flesh, which was blackening like burned parchment.

Matchi pulled the table back just far enough to open the study door. They squeezed through and fled. They could hear the sounds of claws on the floorboards everywhere they ran. Growls and screams echoed through the halls, and they did not know which way to run. The monsters stalked and snarled, then the wind changed direction, and the chapel bell began to ring violently.

As the silver bell tolled the monsters roared and shook their heads, stumbling and slamming against the walls. Claws slashed at the brother and sister as they sped past the agonised creatures. Matchi and Jane ducked past writhing men and women who were buckled with agony as their bones snapped and reformed beneath their skin.

Furred demons and deranged villagers reared from doorways and lunged from dark corridors as Matchi and Jane sprinted through the dark mansion, slamming doors behind them. Matchi, who had so often cursed the sound of the silver bell, now blessed each ringing tone and felt nothing but terror whenever the wind released it long enough for it to fall silent. Without it they were defenceless.

They started down the rear flight of stairs, then had to scramble back as a fully turned monster raced upwards, swift as a wolf from the hall below. Yellow eyes gleaming, jaws wide, it was halfway to them when the bell tolled and it lost its footing and sprawled, spasming on the steps.

'The other way!' Matchi was suddenly glad of all the days spent pacing the mansion. He knew it well, even in darkness, and he dragged Jane by the hand until she was wrenched from his grasp with a scream.

He stumbled a few steps before turning to see her fallen. A beast had the hem of her dress in its jaws and was pulling her into the darkness, shaking its head like a maddened dog. As Jane turned on her back to kick at it, her skirts tore. The beast fell back with a mouthful of cloth and she was free, dragging herself away on her elbows with a half-shredded dress.

The bell tolled again, the monster howled, and Matchi pulled Jane up. There was no time for more than an exchanged glance of terror before they resumed their headlong flight. They descended the front stairs with quick, faltering steps, hoping against hope to find their escape route open.

The front door stood wide and, not knowing where else to go, they ran out into the night. The manor grounds were flooded.

The tide was up to their knees, shocking them with cold as they jumped down the entryway stairs. The sea seemed to pull at them as they started across the courtyard. Then a wave would crash and there would be a sudden surge of waist-high water in the other direction. The water pushed them, stumbling sideways, first one way, and then the other.

The tide would recede briefly, only for another wave to crash into them, and Jane lost her footing on the slick cobbles. She might have been swept away if Matchi was not holding so tightly to her hand. He remembered, with a flash of panic, that Jane did not know how to swim. Then he realised that even the best swimmer could not hope to battle such waves if they were pulled out into the open sea.

A beast lunged at them from the darkness of the old stables and was slammed away by a wave that knocked both Matchi and Jane from their feet. They were helpless for a breath, doused and freezing, and then they had their feet under them again, while the monster was washed howling out to sea.

They struggled through the storm towards the carriage path. Running and kicking up spray when the waves drew back enough to allow it, clinging together when white water buffeted them. They made it past the courtyard wall, and waded along the drowned path, clambering over a fallen tree. Matchi fell, and Jane's hand clamped around his wrist tight as a manacle. She dragged him when he faltered, urging him on, her voice was gentle when he stumbled, nearly hysterical when he begged for rest.

They did not clear the sea until they finally came to the foot of the hill. For a few brief moments Jane let Matchi rest, and he fell down gasping. His lungs were burning and his limbs shaking. He had barely begun to catch his breath when Jane's arm was around his waist, urging him up again. They chose a steep path, dragging themselves up by handfuls of grass and roots, both of them constantly turning to see if there were signs of pursuit. They cowered whenever the bell's ringing ceased and howls sounded through the storm. Slowly they made their way upward, until finally they were above the level of the trees. Jane let Matchi rest. She began to sob and fell to her knees, weeping. Matchi lay still until he could breathe again.

Beneath them the scene was gilded in moonlight as white waves swirled around the mansion. The storm screamed in their ears.

The sound of the silver chapel bell was so thin and distorted by distance that it seemed a single high note in the endless roaring song of the storm.

Upon the backward drag of a huge wave there was a shifting of the land so vast it was vertiginous to watch. There was a deep rumbling beneath their feet and the ground shook. Trees shivered in the forest, then fell like loose twigs. The bedrock upon which La Brecquette Manor stood, tilted and teetered, and was swallowed by the ocean.

Waves roared in around the collapsing land, and the fall of La Brecquette Manor was complete. The silver bell was silenced, and the shape of the coast was altered forever as the tide surged in to claim new territory.

'I hope they were all pulled down with it!' Jane wrapped her brother in hug.

Matchi could only stare, unblinking, as the wind blew tears from his eyes.

'Have you finished the letter, Matchi? Read it to me.' Jane settled herself at the foot of the bed.

Matchi sighed. 'I have told father that he can find us at the Portelet Inn. I have only described the monsters as *wild dogs* so that he doesn't confine us to an asylum. I have written that they ran inside when the flooding began. As for the land, he will have to see the devastation for himself to believe the manor is utterly lost. I've reassured him that I'm staying in bed and that you are looking after me. Look, I have written here: *"Hopefully I will be well enough to travel very soon. Jane did not escape quite unscathed either. When a beast lunged for her, she tore free her skirts from its jaws, but its fangs caught her ankle in a nasty bite. With the fear, and the need to run, she swears she barely felt the pain of the wound at the time. Yet when the sun came up, we saw that her leg was covered in blood. We were concerned about infection, of course, but the physician says the wound is healing unusually fast, so I believe all will be well."'*

Matchi looked up from the letter and asked, 'You aren't feeling any pain, are you Jane?'

His sister slowly smiled.

'No, Brother,' she said softly. 'I have never felt better in my entire life.'

GOBLINS

Till the fuller stream of the might of the tune,
Gliding like a dream in the light of the moon,
Bears them all away, and away, and away,
Floating in the trance of the dance.
Henry van Dyke

It is well known that the collective noun for a flock of crows is a *murder*. It is slightly less well known that ravens, who gather more rarely, are collectively known as a *conspiracy*.

One summer solstice evening, a certain conspiracy of ravens was floating high on the thermals above Mont Orgueil. From their vantage they could see the dark castle, and a sparkling indigo sea. They tilted their wings over the lush green headland and saw ancient dolmen stones, which had been decorated with flowers and lit by lanterns on poles. Near the dolmen people were gathered around a table that held jugs of cider and fresh lemonade. There were plates with little sandwiches, and slices of sweet and savoury pies.

They noticed, without much interest, a pair of slim, swift-walking girls bickering on the way from Gorey Castle to the Faldouët Dolmen, with their chaperone trailing behind them.

'I told you I didn't want to be late, Isobel!' the younger girl said.

'You should be grateful I agreed to bring you to this heathen ceremony at all, Cassie,' her older sister informed her. 'I would not have done so, except that it is so close to the castle.'

Isobel was eyeing the dolmen disapprovingly as they walked towards it. It was a loose oval of large, pale stones, with a giant flat rock balanced improbably at one end.

Cassie sighed. 'It is only Flynn's mother's solstice party. It's not a human sacrificial ceremony. There might even be some dancing. You like dancing, Issy. You know you do.'

'Please do not shorten my name to that appalling diminutive, *Cassiopeia*. I enjoy dancing in ballrooms and country halls like a lady. Not on grassy hilltops around prehistoric stones like a heathen. Please do not pretend that we are here for *any* other reason than your endless infatuation with that wretched fletcher's boy. Stop *rushing*, Cassie. No one ever arrives *on time*. Certainly not with a red face, tripping over the hem of their dress. Making an entrance is important.'

The ravens might have remained disinterested in this little scene had they not also noticed figures moving from the wild woods to the south-west. The smaller figures, while much further away, were moving with determined speed.

The conspiracy of ravens, who had before been spread out across miles of rosy sky, began to draw together, now interested in what might unfold, because while the ravens counted only twelve goblins within this little horde, they could see they were moving with purpose. A humming song emanated from goblin throats, and magic tingled against the tips of the ravens' feathers as the song lifted into the air.

Within the many black chests of these ravens, a single heartbeat kept perfect time. They considered what was unfolding and came to a decision. They were, in every sense, of one mind.

The ravens wheeled and descended, swift as a hurricane. Only one of them broke away from the boiling mass of black feathers that arrowed towards the dolmen on the hill.

'That fiddler would make better music if he lifted up his wretched instrument and started dashing it to pieces on those stones,' Isobel remarked as she sipped lemonade.

Cassie was watching Flynn and his friends over Isobel's shoulder and said, 'Well Lettie is quite the worst dancer I have ever seen, so I suppose the music suits her well. She is so bossy. She always speaks to Bry like…'

With a loud crash that startled everyone, a raven landed upon the trestle table next to the punch and knocked over a jug of lemonade with a lash of one outstretched wing. It walked with determined purpose toward the plates of sandwiches.

This avian incursion into the refreshments resulted in a great deal of loud exclaiming and delighted cries of outrage and amusement from the assembled party. Flynn's mother flapped her apron at the bird. People clapped and shooed. The raven, with fearless audacity, ignored everyone as it selected a cucumber sandwich. It paused a moment with the sandwich in its beak, glared around at everyone, and then leapt back into the sky.

Cassie, laughing with the others, glanced at her sister and saw Isobel was pale, staring at the dolmen with horror. The last drops of lemonade were dripping from the glass which hung loosely from her fingers.

'Issy, are you alright?'

'It was the strangest thing,' Isobel said quietly. 'As that bird landed on the table I saw a whole flock land, behind the dolmen. Where they landed, I thought I saw a man appear. He was dressed all in black. He leant against the dolmen, then I blinked, and he was gone. Except... except I don't think I *did* blink, Cassie.'

Isobel's fingers were trembling so much that Cassie took the empty glass from her and tried to joke gently. 'I've never seen you get unsettled by a man, Isobel. Was he so terribly handsome?'

'What? Yes. I suppose he was. In fact, he was *horribly* beautiful, Cassie. Like something from a dream. He made me feel quite hideous by comparison,' Isobel clasped a hand to her forehead. 'This island! I cannot *stand* it, Cassie. Raven men and glowing white ladies. Monsters in wells and ogres in the woods! It's just not civilised!'

Cassie patted her sister's shoulder in concern. 'Perhaps we did walk too fast. Goodness, Isobel, you have turned so pale! Let's get you some more lemonade.'

Isobel walked after her sister a few shaky steps, then stepped into the cool shadows of the evening to gather herself before anyone could see her so unsettled. She rested her hand against a tree and took a moment to catch her breath as she looked out into the trees.

And so it was Isobel, before all the others, who saw the goblins swarming out of the darkness beneath the trees. She was so shocked to see the strange little men in their barbaric garb that she was unable to gather the breath to scream. Cassie, walking towards her with a glass of lemonade, saw them a moment later and screeched so loudly that the fiddler was startled into a discordant note that stopped his tune.

The goblins moved fast, undeterred by Cassie throwing the glass of lemonade at them in panic. Women screamed and men shouted, and the newly rearranged trestle table was overset entirely with a crash. Goblins sprinted amongst the partygoers, darting here and there.

People were shouting and Isobel heard somebody cry out over and over, 'Goblins! Goblins! Goblins!' but then they fell horribly silent.

At first, with the screaming and running, with people falling and wailing, Isobel thought they were all being killed. She tried to drag Cassie away, and when a grey-skinned goblin lunged towards them, Isobel threw herself in front of her little sister, ready to take a blade in her back.

The goblin had no weapon in its hand. Instead, it grabbed Isobel's wrist for a brief second, slapped at Cassie's bare arm, and leapt away again. Cassie cried out, but there was no pain, only surprise.

Then the sisters tried to move. Isobel met Cassie's gaze with horror and saw her sister was experiencing the same thing that she was. It felt like their limbs were mired in deep mud. Isobel commanded her feet to move, and they did not. She demanded her hands to let go of her sister, but her fingers barely twitched. It took all Isobel's strength just to turn her head a fraction and see that the same thing was happening to people everywhere around the dolmen. The ugly little men were chasing and touching people, who were freezing suddenly where they were. People were trapped in strange poses, their eyes bulging, lips parted in shock. Some were wailing from stupefied mouths, others looked on the verge of falling unconscious.

Isobel was reminded of a children's game, where those who ran and were caught had to remain still. Except the humans did not want to play. Tear-streaked faces were lit by lantern light. The goblins leapt and chased with practised skills.

Isobel's ears tingled uncomfortably, and she did not know why. It felt like snowflakes were falling and melting against her lobes.

'How did you turn your head?' Cassie's teeth were clenched in position as she asked, 'Why is my necklace burning cold?'

'My earrings are doing the same. Oh! I managed to move my foot a little bit. What are these little people? Are they goblins? Somebody was screaming that they were goblins.'

Cassie's eyes went wide, 'Goblins! Wait, Isobel! Perhaps our jewellery feels strange because its silver. Do you remember Flynn saying that silver could defend against some faerie creatures?'

'It was Bry who said that. And I don't feel particularly *defended*. I just feel like I'm wearing cold thistles in my ears.'

'Yes, but look! Most people are quite insensible. I think Lottie is beginning to drool.'

'That does not surprise me in the least,' Isobel said, 'Are the goblins hurting anybody?'

'No, not yet. They chased after the people who ran away down the path though. They're bringing them back and positioning them by the dolmen stones. Do you think they mean to kill us? I apologise if tonight turns into a sacrifice after all. Isobel – *what* is that annoying noise?'

'I don't know, Cassie. I think perhaps those horrid little men are humming for some reason.'

'Shh, one of them is coming over here!'

Isobel felt her hand grabbed by clawed fingers and suppressed a scream as she was led, her legs walking without her consent, in time with the determined stride of the little monster. It was a female, she realised, a little smaller than the others that were grabbing and guiding people towards the dolmen. The little female monster was thin and wiry, with the same big ears and sharp teeth as the others. Her skin was dull yellow, her lean limbs sparsely clothed with rough cut leather and patchwork fabric. She had reddish-gold hair bound up in little feathered tufts and beaded plaits. The creature's eyes were as red as spilled blood. Its glance, as it pulled her into place at the farthest point from the capstone of the dolmen, was without interest.

'Please,' Isobel asked. 'What do you want with us? Please don't hurt my sister!'

The female goblin was already grabbing at somebody else. A leaner, taller goblin with blue skin was dragging Cassie towards the dolmen. Cassie was visibly fighting her steps, while other men and women were walking with placid dreaminess and standing wherever they were left.

Silver, Isobel thought, was keeping them both conscious.

Her earlobes felt as though they had cold nettle rash, but aside from the wiggling of her toes and the flexing of her fingers she might as well have been wrapped in ropes from head to toe. Her thoughts were sluggish, but no more so than if she had drunk a little too much wine.

The goblin humming had a single, stronger voice now, rising and falling. A powerfully built little goblin with green skin had begun singing a wordless, winding song that made the hairs on Isobel's neck stand on end.

'Music, Murk!' The blue goblin squawked.

Drums began to thump and hold a rhythmic beat. A grey male goblin picked up the violin and bow from where the talentless fiddler had dropped them. He pressed them back into the man's hands and shouted, '*Play!*'

The goblin wove a pattern with its fingers and spun and stepped and flexed its arms. It stamped and clenched and pumped its elbows, and the musician, with his eyes unfocused, grasped the bow, lifted the fiddle, and began to make it wail.

Strange music resonated through the warm night air.

'Well, he's improved at least,' Isobel muttered.

The music that poured out of the instrument was vastly different than its owner's previous playing. It rang a counterpoint that drifted and rejoined the song of the green goblin. The grey goblin danced and sung a refrain to complement his green companion. The blue goblin spread his arms in an emphatic gesture, proud as any opera singer, and joined the rising chorus with a light and lilting voice that vibrated in Isobel's bones. He raised an arm and Isobel's arm leapt upward of its own accord. She noticed that every human arm was raised. He nodded and everyone nodded. He dropped his arm and hers fell to her side. Other goblins joined the song and then the goblins danced.

Isobel, with an indignant exclamation, danced too.

All around the dolmen stones the partygoers danced. Their faces registered nothing, their bodies all moved in synchronised motions. They were puppets to the goblin magic. Without wanting to, people danced and leapt and spun.

The music was strange and ugly, yet utterly compelling. One circuit around the dolmen stones the goblins stamped and swirled, some in one direction, the others dancing widdershins. Strange shadows leapt in flickering lantern light. Isobel's body flexed and spun. Her hands lifted and her feet stepped swiftly. She turned in the opposite direction without ever having decided to do so and winced as half of the partygoers changed direction to weave dancing through the other half, but somehow there were no collisions.

This was not the courtly dancing she had learned with her French instructor. This was a stamping, tribal rigorous exertion. Isobel soon realised that she was expending twice the energy by fighting her own limbs and achieving nothing from the battle, except a few twitches and missteps. There was more likelihood of wrenching a muscle, or dislocating an arm, than bringing her body back under control. The easiest thing to do, was nothing, letting her body perform the movements already chosen for her.

Cassie was in the group moving in the opposite direction. They saw each other each time they passed.

'Why are we dancing?' Cassie whispered, and then as they passed again. 'How I *wish* I'd worn different shoes!'

'Flynn!' Isobel saw the young man that was the object of Cassie's infatuation dance past. He looked terrified, but awake. Isobel could see he was wearing a silver necklace. The magic of the goblins clearly intoxicated and confused those under its spell, and only Isobel, Cassie, Flynn and an old, weeping woman were astute enough, or wearing enough silver, to be fully aware of what was happening to them.

'The legends,' Flynn gasped as they passed each other in a whirl of arms.

'What legends?' Isobel asked as they passed again.

'Madame Auffroy is sound asleep,' Cassie informed her, stamping past.

Flynn's expression was grim as he danced towards her again.

'Everybody knows the legends of goblins making people dance themselves to death!' he whispered harshly as he passed.

His words made her blood turn cold. She realised that the light was altering. The pale dolmen stones had begun to take on a violet tinge. At first Isobel thought they might be beginning to glow.

Isobel realised her limbs were aching far more than they should for the exertion she had expended. She was young, and healthy and walked almost every day. Living in a castle meant she was constantly running up and down stairs. Yet she felt drained, like she had been running for miles.

'Didn't I say there might be dancing?' Cassie said with a tremulous smile as they drew level for a moment. Isobel could see that her sister's lashes were wet with tears, so she smiled through her own fear.

As she danced behind the capstone of the dolmen Isobel realised that the weak, purple light was coming from violet shadows. They were rising from the breath of the dancers like steam, drifting upwards to hang in a sparkling cloud.

Isobel began to be truly afraid. Flynn's blond hair was sticking to his brow with perspiration.

'They're pulling something out of us!' he said.

'*Life*,' Isobel said softly once he was out of earshot.

Isobel tried to fight her traitorous limbs again, to make her body do anything other than dance, but she was no more successful than the last time. The goblins singing together were too strong. No amount of will or physical strength could defy the magic that was puppeting her body.

The thin blue goblin slipped through the dancers and urged the yellow female goblin towards the dolmen.

'Now, Claw. *Make.*'

The little monster nodded. She jumped into the oval of stones and scuttled under the giant capstone. Settling herself cross-legged she began to sing again, weaving her fingers in strange shapes. Her elbows pumped along with the dance. As her hands moved, the purple light began drifting towards her, seeming to thicken and gain substance as she reached for it. It wound about her arms, brightening and becoming more concentrated at a single point.

The yellow goblin's red eyes rolled back in her head.

Isobel could see the soft purple light as she breathed out, and feared that it might mean years of her life were being stolen away. She fought back tears, determined not to let her little sister see her scared.

'Do you think we're going to die?' Cassie asked her, as she danced past. Cassie's face was grey, with dark circles beneath her eyes as though she had not slept for a week. She sobbed, then let out a little scream when a whirl of ravens suddenly exploded from the capstone of the dolmen like a hurricane. Their black feathers looked rich, dark purple as they were lit by the Goblin magic. They flapped within the oval of stones, a living swirl of black. Then the swirl became a black cloak, and a tall, slender man threw back his hood and stood, with raised brows and a sinister smile.

Cassie was gaping with astonishment.

As Isobel passed her sister, she said shakily, 'You see, Cassie? I told you making an entrance is important.'

'Lord Regent!' Two of the goblins broke from the dance and leapt inside the stones, shielding the yellow goblin with their bodies.

The other goblins continued the song though, and despite her efforts, Isobel continued to dance. The man the goblins called Regent looked down with a mocking smile.

'Is this a party, Greem?' his voice was as smooth and cold as a knife slipping into a heart, 'If so, why was I not invited?'

'Not *party*, no Lord,' the taller goblin answered.

Both were cowering slightly, and Isobel noticed all the other goblins had wary eyes fixed on the fae lord as they danced. Isobel eyed the Regent hopefully but doubtfully. He looked every inch a faery prince, but not of the good kind. Flynn looked white as death.

'Is *that* who you saw?' Cassie whispered when she passed her by.

The Regent jumped up onto a dolmen stone with easy grace and spun, arms out, gesturing to the humans who were leaping and twirling like broken puppets around him.

'If this isn't a party, whatever are you *doing*, Blu?' He demanded.

'We make *key*, Lord.'

The one called Greem punched the one called Blu in the arm. Then they both fidgeted awkwardly.

'Oh, was it a secret?' The Regent asked, stirring the purple light that was clouding above his head with a pale finger. 'So you're making a stone key. How *very* ambitious of you. May I ask why you want one?'

Isobel exchanged a baffled look with Cassie as they passed.

'Lord,' the thin blue goblin wrung his hands. 'Only most *powerful* have key. Key is power. Key is *treasure*.'

'So we *want* one,' the other goblin said firmly.

The Regent sighed and hopped down from the stone, 'That makes a goblin sort of sense I suppose.'

He leaned over the two goblins and they crept backward.

'Now explain,' said the Regent softly, 'Why you have broken the covenants. Explain why you are interacting with humans, when you know it is *forbidden*.'

There was such a weight to the last word that all the goblins flinched and the humans under their control flinched too.

'Lord,' the goblin called Greem leaned so far back from the Regent that he ended up sitting down, 'We try before now. Make key with *shadow numbness*, but...'

'Too hard. Not enough magic,' Blu said. He pointed at the dancers. 'We steal some.'

'I understand,' the Regent sighed.

'You *not* stop goblins?' Greem asked suspiciously.

'Not at all,' the Regent stood straight and shrugged, 'Why would I? A few paltry human lives… What possible difference could they make to me?'

'Thank you, Lord,' the goblins bowed, first one, then the other.

'Murk!' Blu barked, 'Help Claw!'

The grey goblin vaulted into the oval. He bowed to the Regent awkwardly, bowed again, then backed away towards the capstone. He faced Claw and began to dance furiously. His hands gathered purple light as he spun and stamped, and he pushed the light onwards to the female goblin. Isobel felt a wave of exhaustion and despair. She would have fallen if the magic wasn't holding her up.

'Claw has *strongest* magic,' Blu said to the Regent, gesturing at the little yellow goblin, then he asked again, 'You not *stop* goblins?'

'I wouldn't dream of it,' said the Regent gently.

Blue nodded leaping back into the dance, and Greem moved to follow. Then the green goblin suddenly spun, gripped with awful suspicion, and shouted, 'Don't steal key, Lord!'

'Why would I want your key?' The Regent asked, lifting his brows curiously.

Greem wrung his hands, 'Because key *treasure*! Don't take key, Lord. Promise. Not stop goblins! Not steal key!'

'I give you my word. I am actually *very* curious to see if you can create one without killing yourselves.' He smiled and then added, 'However, I did feel obliged to go and inform the White Lady what you are doing. This is a flagrant disregard of the agreements, after all.'

'Sneak!' Greem shouted, appalled.

Like the sun coming out from behind a cloud the White Lady stepped away from the capstone. In the night she glowed. She had an expression of severe displeasure as she turned to take in the scene.

Isobel felt a flood of hope and saw an expression of joy on her sister's exhausted face as she danced past. Even though his body still danced and stamped, Isobel suspected Flynn had fainted. All of the other dancers seemed unconscious, and Isobel wondered, with a little flash of horror, whether they were already dead. The idea of corpses dancing around her was too revolting to dwell upon.

'What is the meaning of this?' *La Blianche Danme*'s voice was clear as a struck bell.

'We make key!' Greem shouted and then jumped into the dance.

The White Lady looked profoundly confused.

'I believe the problem,' the Regent suggested, eyes glittering with amusement, 'Is that our little friends don't really understand what stone keys are. However, they have decided they are valuable. They are 'treasure'. They didn't have enough power to make one without help... So, they decided to do things in the old way.'

'Wretched goblins,' said the White Lady in exasperation.

She stepped out of the stone oval and pulled the old woman from the dance, laying her down and touching her forehead with a single finger.

'Sleep,' she said, and the old woman fell still.

'Is she dead?' Cassie cried out.

'No,' the White Lady said, 'although she soon would have been.'

'Can you *please* help us, my Lady?' Isobel asked softly as she danced past. 'This is *so* undignified.'

'Not stop goblins!' Blu shouted.

'We wants key!' *You* has key. *You* has key,' Greem pointed first at the White Lady and then at the Regent, and then stamped a foot that was echoed in movement by human dancers, 'Goblins important! Goblins get key!'

'If you won't stop, I will have to make you stop,' The White Lady said, and green shoots began to grow and creep around the dolmen stones. 'Reverse this magic *now*. I will not allow you to kill these people.'

'*Can't* stop key. Too late,' Murk shook his head as he danced.

'Key is ours! Ours for *us*!' Blu danced past her.

The Regent's smile grew to a grin as the White Lady raised her hands in disbelief.

'They are not *treasure*, Blu. Undo this.'

'Can't,' said Greem dancing past. 'Don't know how. Too late.'

'The little idiot may have a point,' the Regent interjected. 'Breaking the magic now would probably release enough shadow numbness to stupefy the island for days. It would certainly kill the female Goblin. I wonder if she would explode. It might be better to let these idiots finish. Here, let me speed things along...'

The Regent lifted a flat palm and exhaled a shadow into the cloud of purple, as if he was blowing black dust. Rich dark magic coiled like smoke and darkened the violet strands that the yellow goblin was feeding into the point of light, which grew suddenly brighter and began to take on form.

'You are right, of course,' sighed the White Lady. 'How *very* annoying of you. Let's finish this before someone dies.'

She lifted her arms and light blazed.

The purple light rippled as white energy tore through it, refracting rainbows and humming with power. The yellow goblin's singing became a panicked shouting. Her yellow claws flicked almost too fast to see. Goblins sang and danced, human bodies twirled once more, and with a pulse of purple power that knocked the humans and goblins onto the ground, it was finished.

Not everyone had fallen, Isobel realised. The Regent and the White Lady were standing, unaffected and unimpressed, looking at what had been created.

The yellow goblin sat up, clenching something that looked like a flat, dark pebble in triumph.

'*Stone key!*' she screeched.

'Yes. Now, if...'

The White Lady stopped speaking as the yellow goblin scrambled to her feet, leaped out of the oval of dolmen stones, and sprinted away into the night.

'My key,' the blue goblin said, astonished.

Another goblin shoved him onto the floor and raced after the female.

The other goblins exchanged glances, and then all of them bounded off in pursuit.

'A goblin stone key,' said the Regent watching them go. 'What an absolutely dreadful idea.'

'At least the humans are alive.'

'*Are* they?' The Regent raised an eyebrow at the people laying unconscious around the dolmen.

Isobel stood, shakily, then reeled with exhaustion. She saw Flynn scramble away into the darkness.

Cassie was struggling to sit up.

'What's a stone key?' Cassie asked the White Lady breathlessly.

'What my sister *means* to say is...' Isobel tried to catch her breath. '*Thank you.*'

She started to curtsy, then her unsteady legs buckled, and she slumped down next to Cassie.

'Rest. You will recover from this in a day or so,' the White Lady assured them.

The Regent turned away and tilted his head, 'The goblins are headed for the castle,' he said, sounding amused.

'How do you know that?' Cassie asked, leaning heavily against Isobel.

The White Lady narrowed her eyes suspiciously. 'Why do you imagine Claw is headed for a castle filled with humans?'

The Regent laughed, 'Only consider how goblins think! It's a castle... so there *must* be gold and treasure. Treasure! That little goblin is wielding an item of power, and she plans to try her luck. Queen Claw of Gorey Castle? It has a certain ring to it....'

'The goblins are going to storm the castle?' Isobel put her hand over her eyes. 'Oh dear, I do hope father stays up in the keep where it's safe.'

The Regent gave a relaxed shrug and some ravens flapped away as though they'd been perched on his shoulders. They sped through the night towards the castle, joining others that were already in the sky. From high above the ravens saw a swift little yellow goblin sprinting through the castle gate. The sleepy men guarding it shouted in surprise and failed to stop her. As they panicked and turned to chase her, they left the gate unprotected. The rest of the little horde of goblins raced in behind them.

One of the soldiers was knocked down and trampled in their rush. By the time the other man had drawn his sword, the goblins were already out of reach. The Regent laughed softly as he watched through raven eyes and heard the cries of men who were startled by the sight of goblins running through the shadows of the castle's lower ward.

'Do I need to intervene?' The White Lady asked the Regent.

'I don't believe so, my Lady. It's far too dark for the humans to see the goblins clearly. They have no idea what is happening. What *is* Claw doing...?'

His ravens glided over the castle walls, watching as areas of confused chaos broke out across the grounds of the castle. Such a tiny invasion had never been imagined or prepared for, and most of the castle's defenders had retired to bed for the night. Disbelief and incredulity slowed any hope of a meaningful response to the small horde of goblins rampaging through the darkness.

Holding the stone key high, Claw was headed up the long stone staircase towards the middle ward. The Regent watched, through the eyes of a conspiracy of ravens, and related the activity he saw taking place.

'From what I can see, the key does wield the shadow numbness of goblin magic, but it has limited power,' he said, 'It seems it can only control a single person at a time. At this moment, one of the human swordsmen is enchanted. He is defending Claw, much against his will, from another human soldier. The little goblin looks rather disappointed. She was probably hoping to have the entire castle under her power by now. Some of the other goblins are ransacking the human food stores. They are creatures of havoc. I am almost fond of them. Blu, Murk and Greem have followed Claw up towards the middle ward. There are guards descending from the keep now, so Claw has retreated to hide in the well cave.'

'Oh dear,' whispered Cassie to Isobel. 'She shouldn't go in there at this time of night. There's probably still that *cocangne* monster living in there, and she is the size of a child.'

'Serve her right if she gets eaten,' said Isobel. 'I hope they *all* get eaten, the horrid things. I have never felt more exhausted in my entire life, and I am all in disarray. I really... I think I must lay down.'

She lay, head spinning, listening to the fée lord and lady as they talked.

'Ah, it appears from their arguing,' said the Regent, 'that they have dropped the stone key down the well, by accident.'

'Of *course* they have,' sighed the White Lady. 'Are they trapped in the castle now?'

'I don't believe so,' the Regent shook his head, 'The goblins up on the middle ward are already going over the wall. Goblins are excellent climbers. Those on the lower ward have knocked down the guards again and are heading out the same way they came in. And they've stolen everything they can carry.'

The Regent blinked twice, shifted his focus, and looked at the White Lady with a smile.

'What a magnificent evening!' he declared. 'I am always such excellent company.'

The White Lady shook her head at him in amused disbelief, then turned to look at all the unconscious humans sprawled around the dolmen. She compressed her lips.

'I believe the goblins must be punished for this,' she said slowly.

'Shall we kill them?' The Regent tilted his head.

'Oh no, I have thought of a far more apt punishment...' There was a wicked gleam in her eyes as she asked. 'Since you see so much, Lord Regent... Have you ever seen where the goblins bury their treasure?'

'It's at *Le Câtillon*,' said the Regent promptly, pointing to the south-west. 'Their hoard is enormous though. They've been building it for centuries. Are you planning to *steal* it? Whatever will you do with a cartload of coins and goblin gold?'

'Oh, I don't *want* it. I don't need to *steal* it to take it away from them,' the White Lady moved an elegant hand slowly from right to left and said. 'I'm just intending to *move* it a little bit... so that the goblins *believe* it has been stolen.'

The Regent laughed, then looked mildly suspicious. 'I hope I am not expected to dig any holes? I am always far too well dressed for physical labour. Rabbits perhaps...'

The White Lady twirled a finger and tiny briar roses began to grow and bloom around the base of the dolmen stones.

'You need not lift a finger, my Lord,' she smiled. 'Just show me where the treasure is, and I will send roots to entangle it and move it beneath the earth.'

The Regent clapped his hands together and said, 'An excellent idea! I always prefer plans where I am not expected to do anything.'

He tilted his head then and frowned. 'The boy that ran away has now alerted the castle to our presence. Soldiers are making their way here to help their people. And possibly embarrass themselves trying to kill us. Shall we depart before their arrival? Or shall we stay and wish them solstice greetings?'

The White Lady laughed and turned to the two girls.

'It seems assistance is on the way,' she said. 'I must bid good night to you, young ladies.'

Isobel made a slight effort to get up, but the White Lady waved her down, and so the sisters bid the fée lord and lady a tired farewell from the ground.

The Regent gave the barest suggestion of an acknowledgement before he touched the capstone and disappeared.

Cassie quickly asked, 'My Lady. Before you go... will you *please* explain what a stone key is?'

The White Lady shook her head. 'I am afraid that is a very long story.'

She smiled at them.

And then she was gone.

AUTHOR'S NOTES ON THE TEXT

A few of the stories in this collection are retellings of existing legends, but most are inspired by partial tales, or the names, locations and descriptions of monsters from local folklore. For those who are interested, I wanted to provide a very brief summary of the existing mythology used within the stories.

La Cocangne in Jèrriais translates to 'well monster', although the spelling varies. It seems likely they were used as a warning to children, to ensure they kept a safe distance from the edge of water. There is a place named La Cocagne on the north coast of Jersey, which is a small rocky waterfall and pool. It is also likely that a monster of this sort was believed to have resided in a large pond in the area near Rue de Cocagne in the east of Guernsey.

The Mermaid is a retelling of a surprisingly little-known legend in Jersey, *The Mermaid's Comb*, which has variations that are told in towns along the southwest coast of Britain. In some versions, and locations, the mermaid leads her saviour to a lost treasure by way of thanks. In some she warns him of the threat of a great wave, enabling him to save his village. Often, but not always, the legend is told as a love story, and usually includes the magic comb.

Black Dogs. Where most monsters of the Channel Islands suffer from a scarcity of information, the absolute opposite is true of the black dogs. In Guernsey, as the story reflects, there are many accounts of black dogs that vary and contradict. Different behaviours and descriptions are attributed to dogs in different areas. The story in this book evolved as much from the contradictions and uncertainties in the source material, as from the various black dogs described within it.

L'Êmânue has the opposite problem. It had been almost forgotten, and thus is described very vaguely. Possibly it was a large 'invisible beast' but also it is remembered as being 'grotesque'. When stories are no longer told, recollections grow thin, leaving us with an 'invisible beast' that had almost entirely disappeared. For illustrative purposes, our *L'Êmânue* was a monster hidden in plain sight, rather than being truly invisible. The story evolved from the nature of its camouflage.

Kelpies have three legends that are intact and entire. In the Guernsey story of the *Fifteen Drunk Men and a Kelpie*, the riders were very fortunate not to end up drowned or eaten alive, since the kelpies of the Channel Islands are usually vicious sea creatures. In the forests of Ireland and England, kelpies are freshwater monsters who linger by deep dark pools. They usually appear as black horses. The kelpies of Bonne Nuit Bay in Jersey are said to be white, however.

La Vioge, as a legend, would probably have been lost to time were it not for the very steep and pretty little footpath named after it. La Ruette à la Vioge can be found in St Peter, Jersey. *La Vioge* is incarnated here in the form of a scarecrow, which is one old description given of the monster's likeness. Very little else remains of its legend, except that it had a cave lair where it would take its victims. The word '*vioge*' itself seems to translate to 'weariness'.

Hearth Faeries can be found worldwide and seem to have been considered common in the islands. Guernsey has a legend of *Le Grand Colin and Le Petit Colin*, who a housewife heard talking one day as they used her oven to bake their bread. The faery bakers would leave a fresh loaf as thanks each time they baked. When the wife told her husband what was happening, he tried to spy on the Colins. The faeries were so offended that they moved out, and there was no more faery bread for the couple.

La Blianche Danme has a road named after her, and she is connected with the dolmens and pouquelaye standing stones of Jersey. She is generally considered a benevolent or protective figure. Accounts of the White Lady are frequent, but sparse, and suggest that at some point in history she was very widely known, before being almost entirely forgotten. *Lé barbou*, who appears in her story, is also a monster from local legend, remembered as some kind of large and unpleasant ogre or troll.

Shapeshifters is a story inspired by the vast number of Channel Island myths of black animals suddenly growing huge and causing chaos or playing strange and senseless tricks. As times changed, old stories and tales of misfortunes that would once have been attributed to faery mischief, were now believed to be devilry, or witchcraft. The wicked or mischievous faery, who had tricked and beguiled people in the old tales, became the devil himself (*lé dgiâbl'ye* or *lé dain*). The story includes *la vielle d'avoût*, the air sprite, or wind goddess, blamed for the often-seen little whirlwinds of petals, sand or dust in the islands. *Les mannes' á fou* are referenced in the folklore as a now forgotten type of invisible, or imaginary, collection of monsters.

Dragons have one very famous legend in the island; the Hambie Dragon's famous battle at La Hougue Bie, which can be found in the book *Jersey Legends*. Castle Cornett in Guernsey was indeed partially destroyed in 1671 by an absurdly accurate lightning strike into the area where the munitions and gunpowder were stored, but whether or not a dragon was involved is entirely for the reader to decide.

Lé Bélengi and *faeu bélenger* legends are very similar to the common will-o'-the-wisp legends found worldwide of lost people following a blue light through wetlands. Jersey's was located in St Lawrence. The *faeu bélenger* in Guernsey is rumoured to have electrocuted a man who got too close to it, which is entirely unique behaviour for a wisp, as is its manner of roaming the beaches near Vale Castle, rather than marshland.

Les P'tits Faîtchieaux are the smaller-sized faery creatures within the islands but vary enormously in type. The story about Les Grîngnolles dé la Niet was inspired by the genuine fear of some islanders as late as the 1920s that opening and uncovering the dolmens was tantamount to digging up faery barrows, and therefore bound to have terrible consequences. Les Grîngnolles were believed to be either dark faeries or shadowy evil spirits who were trapped in the buried stones.

Lé Croque-Mitaine translates as Crooked Faery. 'Mitaine' is another local name for usually dark or wicked faeries in the islands. Parents would sometimes threaten children who misbehaved that the Crooked Faery would come to punish them. The Crocque-Mitaine has only a few details recorded in local sources, but *Blackwood's Guide to Dangerous Fairies* describes the species as a French 'child-thief' known for hiding under beds in the winter, sometimes biting off noses and toes.

Changelings are a very common horror myth worldwide, and the basic legend varies very little. A human baby will be replaced by a faery shapeshifter. The faery baby then gives itself away, either through speech or behaviour. Sometimes a threat to the changeling is enough to make the creature's mother return and replace the human child. Sometimes the human mother is thought to have gone mad for claiming that the changeling is not her baby. The best-recorded changeling legend from Guernsey is related within the story by the character of Emma Le Brocq.

Revenants contains a few myths around the area of Ouaisne Bay, Jersey, which was a haven for smugglers and pirates. Ghouls are a common legend throughout Europe, monsters that lurk in graveyards. The Woman in Black is an established old Jersey ghost story. The woods at Pointe le Grouin were supposedly the planned site of St Brelade's church, until the Faeries took offence and moved the chapel along the coast. The tchéziot (various spellings are used), or 'devil's deputy' is recorded in local folklore as a shadowy creature who can summon dark forces at will.

Les Syraines of Sorel Point is a tale of Lé Prince and La Prîncêsse, who were mythic ship-wreckers. Once they had lured ships onto the rocks, the prince would conduct a trial for the survivors. He would always find them guilty, of course, and then murder them. There is an overlapping legend of Eune Syraine, a siren who lures sailors to their deaths with singing, but whether this is definitely La Prîncêsse, or an alternative myth, is not entirely clear.

Storm Witches is a story similar to two legends of the Witches' Rock in St Clement, Jersey: the tale of Hubert and Madelaine, which appears in *Jersey Legends*, and the much better-known *Tale of the Thirteenth Fish* in which fishermen had to give the thirteenth fish of their catch to pass safely by the storm witches, or else the weather would suddenly turn to a hurricane, destroying their boats.

Les Loups-Garous is inspired by legends of l'ouathou and le loup-garou, which are standard werewolf folklore within the Channel Islands. I included the (possibly semi-historical) legend of the fall of La Brecquette manor, said to be owned by John Willis. The manor was apparently located in the area of L'Etacq and backed by forest. When it was swallowed by the sea, people claimed to hear its chapel bell still ringing beneath the waves. The legend is located in the area where ancient, petrified forest is sometimes revealed by the tides.

Goblins of the Channel Islands are described as large for their species. Their folklore connects them with the dolmens and standing stones where they would bury treasure and dance. Anyone who was unlucky enough to be caught seeking their treasure, or who saw them dancing, could be ensorcelled into the goblins' thrall. People were warned to stay away from dolmens, since the goblins would happily dance their victims to death.

ACKNOWLEDGEMENTS

Thanks to all at Jersey Heritage for their support, especially Nicky Lucas and Eve Ozouf. To Nicola Guy for being very, very patient. To Ele Craker, for being a lovely grammar goblin who battled bravely through all the Jersey-French. To Lizzie Martin, without whom, etc. Most of all, thank you Mum, for literally everything. Finally, thank you Amelia Wilde, for the beautiful illustrations that make the monsters more magical than I could ever have hoped for.

Erren Michaels

I'd like to thank my family, in particular my grandparents, for the huge support they gave me, without which I wouldn't ever have been able to do anything. Also my friends and my boyfriend, for keeping me sane enough to work. And, of course, thanks to Erren for giving me the opportunity to draw cool monsters and creatures.

Amelia Wilde